THE SHORT STORY

THE REALITY OF ARTIFICE

STUDIES IN LITERARY THEMES AND GENRES

Ronald Gottesman, Editor
University of Southern California

THE SHORT STORY

THE REALITY OF ARTIFICE

Charles E. May

Twayne Publishers
New York

Maxwell Macmillan Canada
Toronto

Maxwell Macmillan International
New York   Oxford   Singapore   Sydney

Studies in Literary Themes and Genres No. 4

The Short Story: The Reality of Artifice
Charles E. May

Twayne Publishers
Macmillan Publishing Company
866 Third Avenue
New York, New York 10022

Maxwell Macmillan Canada, Inc.
1200 Eglinton Avenue East
Suite 200
Don Mills, Ontario M3C 3N1

Library of Congress Cataloging-in-Publication Data

May, Charles E. (Charles Edward), 1941–
  The short story : the reality of artifice / Charles E. May.
    p.   cm.—(Studies in literary themes and genres ; no. 4)
  Includes bibliographical references and index.
  ISBN 0-8057-0953-3
  1. Short story. I. Title. II. Series.
PN3373.M36   1995   94-32325
809.3'1—dc20   CIP

The paper used in this publication meets the minimum requirements of American National Standard for Information Sciences—Permanence of Paper for Printed Library Materials. ANSI Z3948-1984. ∞™

10 9 8 7 6 5 4 3 2 1 (hc)

Printed in the United States of America

This book is dedicated to my three children:
Hillary, Alex, and Jordan.
They have always given me joy and made me
proud to be a father.

General Editor's Statement

Genre studies have been a central concern of Anglo-American and European literary theory for at least the past quarter century, and the academic interest has been reflected, for example, in new college courses in slave narratives, autobiography, biography, nature writing, and the literature of travel as well as in the rapid expansion of genre theory itself. Genre has also become an indispensable term for trade publishers and the vast readership they serve. Indeed, few general bookstores do not have sections devoted to science fiction, romance, and mystery fiction. Still, genre is among the slipperiest of literary terms, as any examination of genre theories and their histories will suggest.

In conceiving this series we have tried, on the one hand, to avoid the comically pedantic spirit that informs Polonius' recitation of kinds of drama and, on the other hand, the equally unhelpful insistence that every literary production is a unique expression that must not be forced into any system of classification. We have instead developed our list of genres, which range from ancient comedy to the Western, with the conviction that by common consent kinds of literature do exist—not as fixed categories but as fluid ones that change over time as the result of complex interplay of authors, audiences, and literary and cultural institutions. As individual titles in the series demonstrate, the idea of genre offers us provocative ways to study both the continuities and adaptability of literature as a familiar and inexhaustible source of human imagination.

Recognition of the fluid boundaries both within and among genres will provide, we believe, a useful array of perspectives from which to study literature's complex development. Genres, as traditional but open ways of understanding the world, contribute to our capacity to respond to narrative and expressive forms and offer means to discern the moral significances embodied in these forms. Genres, in short, serve ethical as well as aesthetic purposes, and the volumes in this series attempt to demonstrate how this double benefit has been achieved as these genres have been transformed over the years. Each title in the series should be measured against this large ambition.

Ron Gottesman

Contents

Preface

I have been a student and a fan of the short story since I discovered Edgar Allan Poe when I was in junior high school; I have been studying, teaching, and writing about the form for the past twenty-five years. In that time, I think I have learned something about the characteristic way the short story performs that most primal task of "telling a story." Maybe not. Readers of this modest little book will have to determine that. What I have tried to do here is compress and exemplify some of my thinking about the form over the last quarter century.

This book is one in a series that attempts to examine the historical development and generic (that is, genre-related) characteristics of specific literary forms. It follows a format designed to introduce undergraduate and graduate students to the genre, as well as to provide an overview for teachers, critics, and scholars. In accordance with that format, the first chapter is a general analysis of the development of the short story over time; the last chapter is a survey and critique of criticism and commentary. The four chapters that make up the heart of the book tell a somewhat more detailed story about the gradual evolution of the form through its four most important historical and/or generic periods. In each chapter, I have provided critical discussions of important stories representative of each of these periods. The Chronology and annotated list of Recommended Titles are meant to provide an historical and critical framework and to suggest further reading.

Naturally I have developed some of the ideas in this book in earlier studies, and I wish to thank the editors and publishers who gave me an opportunity to publish them. I also wish to thank the following for allowing me to reprint some of this material. Parts of the discussion of Bernard Malamud's "The Magic Barrel" in Chapter 4 first appeared in *Studies in American Fiction,* Fall 1986. Some of the ideas on Hemingway's "Hills Like White Elephants" in Chapter 4 first appeared in my text *Fiction's Many Worlds* (D. C. Heath, 1993); ideas for several of the other stories can be found in the instructor's guide to that book. Some of the discussion of Katherine Anne Porter's "Flowering Judas" in Chapter 4, as well as ideas scattered in Chapter 5, first appeared in *Reference Guide to Short Fiction* (St. James Press, 1993). Finally, some of my ideas on Donald Barthelme, Raymond Carver, and Cynthia Ozick in Chapter 5 were first developed in review articles published in *Magill's Literary Annual* (Salem Press, Inc., 1982, 1989, 1990). I am very grateful to these publishers for their kind permission to reprint this material.

I wish to thank the Scholarly Research Committee of California State University, Long Beach for giving me a summer grant to do the major research for this study. Thanks also to my friend and colleague David Peck at California State University, Long Beach for his conversation and support; to Liz Fowler, former editor at Twayne, for the encouragement to do this book in the first place; to Sylvia K. Miller, current editor at Twayne, for her expert editing; and to series editor Ronald Gottesman, a true "gentleman and a scholar" in the classic sense, for his extremely helpful collegial consultation and advice about the manuscript. As always I owe everything to my mother Kathleen, my father Howard, my wife Pat, and my children Jordan, Hillary, and Alex for their love, encouragement, and support.

Chronology

1885   Birth of Isak Dinesen (d. 1962)

Birth of D. H. Lawrence (d. 1930)

1887   *La Horla*, Guy de Maupassant

Trois Contes, Gustave Flaubert

1888   Birth of Katherine Mansfield (d. 1923)

1890   Birth of Katherine Anne Porter (d. 1980)

1891   *In the Midst of Life: Tales of Soldiers and Civilians*, Ambrose Bierce

Main-Travelled Roads, Hamlin Garland

A New England Nun and Other Stories, Mary Wilkins Freeman

1892   *The Lesson of the Master*, Henry James

The Real Thing and Other Tales, Henry James

1894   *Bayou Folk*, Kate Chopin

Birth of Isaac Babel (d. 1941)

1896   *The Country of the Pointed Firs*, Sarah Orne Jewett

Plain Tales from the Hills, Rudyard Kipling

Birth of F. Scott Fitzgerald (d. 1940)

1897   Birth of William Faulkner (d. 1962)

1898   *The Open Boat and Other Tales of Adventure*, Stephen Crane

1899   Birth of Ernest Hemingway (d. 1961)

Birth of Elizabeth Bowen (d. 1973)

The Monster and Other Stories, Stephen Crane

Birth of Jorge Luis Borges (d. 1986)

1900   Birth of Sean O'Faolain (d. 1990)

Birth of Vladimir Nabokov (d. 1977)

1902   Birth of John Steinbeck (d. 1968)

Youth, a Narrative and Two Other Stories, Joseph Conrad

Desires, John L'Heureux

In the Garden of the North American Martyrs, Tobias Wolff

Sixty Stories, Donald Barthelme

1982   *Shiloh and Other Stories,* Bobbie Ann Mason

The Collected Stories of Isaac Bashevis Singer

1983   *Cathedral,* Raymond Carver

The Collected Stories of Sean O'Faolain

1984   *Family Dancing and Other Stories,* David Leavitt

1985   *Greasy Lake and Other Stories,* T. Coraghessan Boyle

Collected Stories, Tennessee Williams

Back in the World, Tobias Wolff

Later the Same Day, Grace Paley

Darkness, Bharati Mukherjee

The Old Forest and Other Stories, Peter Taylor

1988   *The Middleman and Other Stories,* Bharati Mukherjee

Where I'm Calling From, Raymond Carver

The Emperor of the Air, Ethan Canin

1989   *If the River Was Whiskey,* T. Coraghessan Boyle

The Shawl, Cynthia Ozick

Complete Collected Stories, V. S. Pritchett

1990   *A Place I've Never Been,* David Leavitt

1991   *What Was Mine,* Ann Beattie

Heat and Other Stories, Joyce Carol Oates

Wilderness Trips, Margaret Atwood

Kentucky Straight, Chris Offutt

1993   *The Collected Stories of Reynolds Price*

Chapter 1

OVERVIEW

Mythic Origins

Although there is some justification for the common claim that the short story as a distinct literary genre began in the nineteenth century, the wellsprings of the form are as old as the primitive realm of myth. Studies in anthropology suggest that brief episodic narratives, which constitute the basis of the short story, are primary, preceding later epic forms, which constitute the basis of the novel.

In many ways, the short story, with its usual focus on a single event and a single effect, has remained close to its primal mythic source. Philosophic anthropologist Ernst Cassirer echoes Poe's famous delineation of the short story's singleness of effect in his description of mythical thinking, which, he asserts, also focuses all forces on a single point: "It is as though the isolated occurrence of an impression, its separation from the totality of ordinary, commonplace experience produced not only a tremendous intensification, but also the highest degree of condensation."[1]

Philip Wheelwright confirms this similarity by reminding us that the mythopoeic outlook most often is represented in the

1

form of particular concrete narratives. A myth not only expresses the inner meaning of things, says Wheelwright, but it does so specifically, by telling a story.[2] Just as the religious experience begins in momentary perceptions of spirit that later become conceptualized into structured theological frameworks, the short story begins in momentary perceptions of what Mircea Eliade calls the "sacred," which later accumulate and become conceptualized into the organized narrative form we have come to know as the novel.[3] Russian formalist B. M. Éjxenbaum makes the distinction emphatic: "The novel is a syncretic form (whether its development be directly from collections of stories or complicated by the incorporation of manners-and-morals material); the short story is a fundamental, elementary (which does not mean primitive) form."[4]

As Cassirer and Eliade define the terms, the "mythic" or "sacred" motivation for short narrative persisted throughout the Middle Ages. In England, for example, from the seventh through the fourteenth centuries, most short verse narratives such as *Genesis B*, *Exodus*, *Judith*, and *The Dream of the Rood* take their narrative materials from Judeo-Christian myth and their moral purpose from Judeo-Christian theology. The romance form, dominant at the turn of the thirteenth century, is represented in short fiction by such exemplary narratives as "Athelston" and "Sir Orfeo," which were used to illustrate moral points in medieval sermons. Although this medieval form of short fiction in verse survived into the Renaissance, in the fifteenth century the short narrative shifted from poetry to prose and its purpose shifted from moral edification to entertainment; one example of such narratives is the French *lai*, which often was used for adapting folklore motifs to the chivalric social milieu. But even when the moralities disappeared, supernatural elements—either from religious myth or from folklore—persisted in these short fictions, even as their focus was slowly "displaced" toward everyday reality by their accommodation to evolving social contexts.

Short Narratives from the Renaissance to the Age of Romanticism

Boccaccio, of course, is the central figure in this gradual displacement of the religious toward the secular in Renaissance short fiction. Nineteenth-century literary historian Francesco De Sanctis argued that *The Decameron* marks a shift from the sacred world of Dante's "divine comedy" to the profane world of Boccaccio's "human comedy." Whereas the basic quality of the literature of the Middle Ages was transcendence to a sort of "ultrahuman and ultranatural 'beyond'" outside of nature and man, Boccaccio devoted himself to the events of everyday life. With him, says De Sanctis, the world of the spirit was replaced by the world of nature. God and Providence as determinants of action gave way to chance, and thus, De Sanctis argues, "a new form of the marvelous was born, not from the intrusion into life of certain ultranatural forces, such as vision or miracles, but by the extraordinary confluence of events which could not be foreseen or controlled."[5]

Boccaccio's stories do mark a shift from the realm of the sacred to the profane world of everyday reality, but they are not "realistic" in the way that we now understand that term. Characters in Boccaccio's stories are not "as-if-real" people in a similitude of the real world; rather, they are primarily functions of the stories in which they appear. Moreover, Boccaccio presents himself in *The Decameron* not as an observer and transcriber of real life but as a collector and teller of formalized traditional tales.

An exemplar of the next phase of short fiction's development can be found in Cervantes, who *does* present himself as an inventor of original stories; his short narratives derive more from his direct observation than from traditional tales, and he records concrete detail in more profusion than did Boccaccio. Moreover, characters are more important in Cervantes's short *Exemplary Novels* than in Boccaccio's *The Decameron*, for their actions can be attributed to psychological motivation based on observation of "real" people rather than to aesthetic motivation based on formulaic functions in traditional stories.

This shift of short fiction's focus from the supernatural to the natural was further carried out in the seventeenth century through developments that moved the form closer to the narrative method that Ian Watt and others have called eighteenth-century "realism."[6] Charles Mish says that two such basic modernizing trends took place in short fiction in England from 1660 to 1700 as a result of French influence: a rising interest in psychological analysis and in *vraisemblance,* or verisimilitude. Mish says that, as a result of these trends in such works as Mme de Lafayette's *Princess de Cleves* (1678), by the end of the seventeenth century, fiction in England was rapidly moving toward the eighteenth-century novel.[7] In fact, short fiction was almost completely replaced by the novel during this period—the notable exception being short fiction's resurgence for purposes of edification, albeit in the service of social rather than religious values. As Benjamin Boyce observes, eighteenth-century authors seem to have no clear conception of short fiction as a genre except perhaps as the sort of narrative-based essay, in which the primary virtue is instruction in social values, that appeared in Addison and Steele's *The Spectator*.[8]

Daniel Defoe's "A True Relation of the Apparition of One Mrs. Veal" is perhaps the paradigmatic example of eighteenth-century short fiction's midway position between the narrative essay presented to teach a moral lesson and the realistic story developed for its own sake, as an account of an actual event. In discussing the conventions of this "marriage of realism to didacticism" in "A True Relation," Edward W. Pilcher has noted the importance of Defoe's establishing the credentials of the teller and assuring the reader that the events described actually took place in such *Spectator*-type narratives.[9] Defoe's story, in addition to being cited as an early example of both the old moral tale and the new narrative of verisimilitude, has also been called a precursor of the Gothic mode that dominated English short fiction later in the eighteenth century. It attempts to validate, by means of the techniques of realism, the appearance of the kind of ghostly apparition that before the eighteenth century might well have been accepted in folktales as an article of belief and faith.[10] "A True Relation" therefore looks both backward to the traditional fable, presented to teach a moral lesson, and forward to the realistic story, presented as an account of an actual event.

Although there are Gothic elements in Defoe's tale, the true Gothic narrative, which was later to have such a powerful influence on the beginnings of the short story in America, began in Germany with Goethe, E. T. A. Hoffmann, Heinrich Kleist, Ludwig Tieck, and A. W. Schlegel—critics and creators of the *novelle*, a short form that combined elements of folktale and realism by focusing on a marvelous happening that at the same time was conceivable. The basic difference between the novel and the *novelle*, German critics have argued, is that characters in the novel develop through time as they are conditioned or determined by their milieu, whereas the *novelle* presents characters who are already developed and are brought into a conflict that reveals them. Although its focus on a particular case biased the *novelle* toward a realistic depiction, the very shortness of the form required the high degree of formalization characteristic of the folktale.

Nineteenth-century French short fiction, beginning with Prosper Mérimée's "Mateo Falcone," marks a movement away from the eighteenth-century *conte philosophique* of Voltaire and the romantic return to folktale; the basic difference, however, is that the new romantic treatment of the stuff of the old tales focused on the subjective inner world of dreams and hallucinations that originally had given rise to the tales. As French writers moved away from the presentation of external descriptions to the interior portrayal of character, the plots in their stories shifted from the presentation of a sequence of events toward an emphasis on a character's reaction to events. As with the German *novelle*, this also marks a shift from a realistic narrative, which presents character gradually developing within a social milieu through time, toward a revelatory narrative that focuses on characters in isolation experiencing basic existential conflicts.

The romantics attempted to demythologize folktales, to divest them of their external values, and to remythologize them by internalizing those values and self-consciously projecting them onto the external world. They wished to preserve the old religious values of the romance and folktale without their religious dogma and supernatural trappings. Understanding that stories were based on psychic processes, they secularized the mythic by foregrounding their subjective and projective nature. The folktale, which previously had existed seemingly in vacuo, as a received story not influenced by the teller, became infused with the subjectivity of the poet and projected onto the world as a new mythos. Value existed in the external world, but, as the romantics never forgot, only because it existed first within the imagination of the artist. Just as the uniting of folktale material with the voice of an individual perceiver in a concrete situation gave rise to the romantic lyric, as Robert Langbaum has shown, the positioning of a real speaker in a concrete situation, encountering a specific phenomenon that his own subjectivity transforms from the profane into the sacred, gave rise to the short story.[11]

Irving, Hawthorne, Poe

Washington Irving's focus on tone rather than incident illustrates this new emphasis on the teller and accounts for the combination of attitudes that come together to create the short story
in America. While Irving did take as his subject matter the stuff
of folklore, it is the point of view or "voice" of his teller that sets
his stories apart from the Germanic models from which he bor-
rowed the situations of "Rip Van Winkle" and "The Legend of
Sleepy Hollow." In a letter to Henry Brevoort in 1824, Irving
wrote, "I consider a story merely as a frame on which to stretch
my materials. It is the play of thought, and sentiment and language; the weaving of characters, lightly yet expressively delineated; the familiar and faithful exhibition of scenes in common
life; and the half-concealed vein of humor that is often playing
through the whole—these are among what I aim at."[12]

Both Fred Lewis Pattee and Edward J. O'Brien in their 1923
histories of the American short story place the birth of the form
with Washington Irving's combination of the style of Addison
and Steele's essays with the subject matter of German romanticism. Pattee says of Irving's *Sketchbook*, "It is at this point where
in him the Addisonian Arctic current was cut across by the Gulf
Stream of romanticism that there was born the American short
story, a new genre, something distinctively and unquestionable
our own in the world of letters."[13] Focusing more on the classical
"Arctic" than on the Gulf Stream romanticism, O'Brien says that
the short story begins with the *Sketchbook* when Irving detaches
the story from the essay, especially the personal essay of the
eighteenth century which arose from the need to chronicle the
"talk of the town."[14]

Diedrich Knickerbocker, the narrator in Irving's two most
famous stories, is more like the eighteenth-century "town talker"
Roger de Coverly memorialized by Addison and Steele than like
the anonymous storyteller of folktale. Whereas in the folktale the
personality of the teller seldom intrudes, the town talker emphasizes his own personal impression of that which he narrates and
describes. If Irving's *Sketchbook*, especially "The Legend of Sleepy
Hollow" and "Rip Van Winkle," mark a significant departure,
that innovation lies in his uniting of traditional folktales with the
individualized narrator: while maintaining interest in the events

of the story, he adds another, subjective interest in the story's point of view.

However, it is with Hawthorne's and Poe's development of the romantic impulse that the short story truly begins in America. Poe's contribution, says H. S. Canby in his early history of the form, was to do for the short story what Coleridge and Keats were doing for poetry—to excite the emotions, and to apply an impressionistic technique to his materials in order to hold his stories together. Poe's attempt to convey a "single impression of a mood, or emotion, or situation, to the reader," was a distinguishing characteristic of short fiction.[15] However, according to Canby, Hawthorne places a moral situation at the nucleus in order to give narrative shape to his stories. He was the first American story writer to build a story on an active relationship between characters and circumstances.

However, such an "active relationship" does not unequivocally create a "realistic" story. Indeed, much of Hawthorne's famous "ambiguity" may be due to the fact that many of his stories combine old allegorical conventions with new realistic techniques. Although Hawthorne's most famous story, "Young Goodman Brown," derives from the allegorical tradition, Brown's journey into the forest seems to be prompted by motivations both realistic and allegorical. Moreover, Brown himself seems to be both a character typical of allegory, what Northrop Frye has called a "psychologized archetype," as well as an "as-if-real" character who has his own psychological makeup.[16] Thus, the story manifests a compromise, between realism and allegorical romance, that characterizes the development of short fiction since Horace Walpole's eighteenth-century claim that his Gothic novella *The Castle of Otranto* was an attempt to blend two kinds of romance— the ancient and the modern. "In the former," said Walpole in his famous preface, "all was imagination and improbability; in the latter, nature is intended to be, and sometimes has been, copied with success." Whether he succeeded or not is a matter of some debate, but Walpole's announced intention was to make his characters "think, speak, and act, as it might be supposed mere men and women do in extraordinary situations."[17]

In mid-nineteenth-century America, the drama of the clash of the sacred and the profane took place not in the cosmos or in the lives of the saints or idealized nobles, as in the old romances, but rather in the psyches of the individual, as Hawthorne's and Poe's stories so clearly demonstrate. Alfred C. Ward, in his 1924 study of the modern American and English short story, notes that what links Hawthorne's stories with writers of the twentieth century is that they both "meet in the region of half-lights, where there is commerce between this world and the other world."[18] The difference between short story writers before Hawthorne and those after him is that while this region of half-lights for the preromantic writers exists as part of a mythic belief system and the religious externals of allegory, for writers after the romantic shift it exists within what Henry James has termed Hawthorne's "deeper psychology."

Edgar Allan Poe's most significant contribution to the development of the short story lies in linking his aesthetic concept of unity, derived from the German and English romantics, with his notion of psychological obsession, derived from the Gothic romance. Poe moves the first-person narrator away from the eighteenth-century discursive and distanced ironic voice familiar to readers of the *Spectator* and the stories of Washington Irving, and toward a teller so obsessed with the subject of his narration that the obsession creates the tightly controlled unity Poe discusses in his famous review of Hawthorne's *Twice-Told Tales*. A story unified around a single effect, impression, or impulse is the aesthetic similitude of a psychological obsession: although the story may contain motifs not intrinsically related to the central theme or effect, such details are presented by the author as relatively unbound, motivated by verisimilitude rather than by theme. The reader of such a story, like Poe's famous detective, Auguste Dupin, focuses primarily on those clues or motifs that obsessively revolve around the central effect.

The Rise of Realism

Melville's "Bartleby the Scrivener" marks the next shift in the short story, toward the realism that dominated the form's development for much of the latter half of the nineteenth century. Critic Robert Marler has argued that "Bartleby" is in fact the first "short story," radically different from Hawthorne's and Poe's "tales." While "Bartleby" may indeed mark the beginning of realism, as Marler says, it still maintains the sense of a mysterious romantic underlying significance and suggestiveness, which is not to be found in the realistic novel. The short story, Marler argues, eschews the supernatural and symbols whose primarily function is not *within* the fictive world's natural order. Its brevity forces meaning beneath the surface, where, by the nature of "its indistinctness, it gives the impression of being inexplicable."[19]

Most critics argue that realism, which dominated both European and American literature in the latter half of the nineteenth century, began in Europe with the publication of the first installment of Flaubert's *Madame Bovary* in 1856. However, in his best-known short story, "St. Julian the Hospitaller," Flaubert returns to the medieval saint's legend to find a model for both its character and its form. What makes Flaubert's moral fable different from its medieval source is its foregrounding of the static and frozen nature of the medieval story itself. The real subject matter of Flaubert's story, although it has a moral issue at its center, is the method by which the medieval tale is made moral and illustrative. The events of the story are frozen in timelessness even as the storyteller relates them as if they were occurring in time. By thus laying bare and parodying the old romance conventions, much as Poe did with the Gothic tale, Flaubert established the groundwork for the new realism.

Flaubert was an important influence on the most important nineteenth-century French short story writer, Guy de Maupassant, who in the decade between 1880 and 1890 published over three hundred short stories in a variety of modes. Although he is best known for such surprise-ending tales as "The Necklace" and most respected for such realistic stories such as "Ball of Fat," Maupassant also contributed to the sophistication of the supernatural folktale and the Gothic romance by pushing them even further than did Poe toward the modern mode of psychological obsession and madness. Many of Maupassant's stories, instead of depending on the supernatural, focus on some mysterious dimension of reality justified rationally by the central character. As a result, the reader is never quite sure whether this realm exists in a "marvelous" actuality or whether it is an "uncanny" product of the obsessed mind of the narrator.

Many German critics have argued that short fiction was the ideal form for the movement now called "poetic realism" during the period between the end of romanticism and the beginning of naturalism in Germany—the 1830s through the 1880s. Poetic realism focused on the realm midway between objective truth and the patterned nature of reality, thus uniting realism's emphasis on the multiplicity of things and idealism's conviction of an abstract unity underlying that multiplicity. Basically, poetic realism in Germany was another name for what was being called "impressionism" in France and America. For both movements, what is communicated by the artwork is not simply the subject (as in romanticism) or the object (as in realism) but rather the tone or atmosphere that constitutes the relationship between the subject and the object.

The American short story also became more "realistic" in the late nineteenth century. However, the very fact that during the period from the Civil War until the arrival of Sherwood Anderson's groundbreaking *Winesburg, Ohio* in 1919 the short story was largely in the shadow of the novel in America suggests that the assumptions of realism, and later naturalism, were basically inimical to the conventions of short fiction. Ray B. West has said that naturalism had less of an impact on the short story than on the novel because the shorter form demands more preoccupation with technique than naturalistic writers were willing or able to grant.[20] The basic difference, however, between the romantics and realists—a difference that negatively affected the development of the short story during this period—is their philosophic disagreement about what constitutes significant "reality." For the romantics, what was meaningfully real was the ideal or the spiritual, a transcendent objectification of human desire; for the realists what mattered was the stuff of the everyday physical world.

One of the first results of this shift in focus to everyday realism in American short fiction was the so-called local color movement: for the more a writer focused on the external world, the more he or she emphasized particular places and people, complete with their habits, customs, language, and idiosyncrasies. Whereas it seldom mattered where in the physical world the stories of Hawthorne and Poe took place (they always seemed to take place in the mind of the characters, or in some fabulistic world between fantasy and everyday reality), the stories of Bret Harte were solidly grounded in the American West, just as the stories of Sara Orne Jewett were tied to New England. The realists wished to localize characters in a physical world and to ground their lives in a social reality.

Although the realistic assumption began to predominate in the latter part of the century, romanticism remained; the result was two branches of the local color movement—the earthy western folktale and the eastern sentimental story. Sometimes these two types merged, as they did in the stories of Bret Harte, who managed to combine the sentimental idealism of the East with the humorous realism of the West. Sometimes the conflict between the two types was satirized, as it was in Mark Twain's famous story "The Celebrated Jumping Frog of Calaveras County," in which a western tall-tale artist gets the better of a genteel easterner. Other well-known stories of the period, such as Mary Wilkins Freeman's "A New England Nun" and William Dean Howells's "Editha," expose the sterility of genteel idealism when it is severed from the facts of everyday reality and physical life.

In addition to emphasis on local color, another result of the shift from romanticism toward realism in the latter part of the nineteenth century was a shift in focus, from form to content. For the romantics, pattern was more important than plausibility; thus, their stories were apt to be more formal and "literary" than were the stories of the realists. By insisting on a faithful adherence to the stuff of the external world, the realists had to allow content—which was often apt to be ragged and random—to dictate form. Because of this shift, the novel, which is better able to expand in order to create an illusion of everyday reality, became the favored form of the realists; on the other hand, the short story, basically a romantic form that requires more artifice and patterning, fell to a secondary role.

Poe and Hawthorne knew this difference between the two forms well and, by means of a tightly controlled form, created a self-sustained moral and aesthetic universe in their stories.[21] Those writers of the latter part of the nineteenth century who were committed to the short story form instead of the novel were also well aware of this fact. For example, when Ambrose Bierce entered into the argument then raging between the romantics and the realists, he attacked the William Dean Howells school of realistic fiction by arguing, "to them nothing is probable outside the narrow domain of the commonplace man's most commonplace experience."[22] Bierce was interested in those extreme moments of human experience when reality becomes transmuted into hallucination. His best-known story, "An Occurrence at Owl Creek Bridge," ironically focuses on a real world that seems sterile and lifeless and a fantasy world that seems dynamic and real. It is tight ironic patterning, rather than a slavish fidelity to the ordinary events of the world, that creates the similitude of reality in this story.

Those late-nineteenth-century American writers of the so-called realist school who have had the most influence on the short story in the twentieth century not only wished to present "realistic" content, but were also aware of the importance of technique, pattern, and form. For example, Henry James argued (as Poe had before him) in his influential essay, "The Art of Fiction," that a fictional work is a "living thing, all one and continuous, like any other organism, and in proportion as it lives will it be found . . . that in each of the parts there is something of each of the other parts."[23] Moreover, James argues, a work of art is not a copy of life but far different, "a personal, a direct impression of life." As he makes clear in his notebook entry on his most frequently anthologized story, "The Real Thing," what interests him is the pattern or form of the work—its ability to transcend mere narrative and to communicate something illustrative, something conceptual: "It must be an idea—it can't be a 'story' in the vulgar sense of the word. It must be a picture; it must illustrate something . . . something of the real essence of the subject."[24]

Beginnings of the Modern Short Story

Indeed, it is "impressionism"—an extension of the romantic emphasis on viewpoint and tone introduced by Irving and Poe—that signals the rebirth of the short story at the turn of the century. Many critics have claimed that Stephen Crane marks the true beginning of the modern short story in America. Joseph Conrad, recognizing a kindred spirit, may have been the first to note that it was Crane's impressionism—the combination of the subjectivity of romanticism with the so-called objectivity of realism—that did the most to effect this transition. Conrad wrote in a letter to Crane in 1897: "Your method is fascinating. You are a complete impressionist. The illusions of life come out of your hand without a flaw. It is not life—which nobody wants—it is art—art for which everyone— the abject and the great—hanker—mostly without knowing it."[25]

However, reality in the stories of Stephen Crane does not result from the mere description and narration of events one after the other in a similitude of the temporal structure of the "real world." Rather, the very concept of "reality" is made problematic by moments of time frozen into a kind of spatial stasis by the ironic impression of the perceiver. Crane's unique combination of powerful emotions and ironic observation can be seen clearly in the juxtaposition of objective with subjective points of view in "The Open Boat," in which the narrator seems at once immediately involved and aesthetically detached.

During the latter part of the nineteenth century in America there was also a "return to Poe" by such writers as Frank Stockton and Ambrose Bierce, who focused not on the ragged reality of the everyday but on a formalized aesthetic reality. According to many critics, the most influential source of this formalization of the American short story was O. Henry—a local color writer who so emphasized ironic pattern that his name has become associated with the formulaic short story. O. Henry's popularity and his output was unprecedented: during his career he published over 250 short stories in more than thirty-four different magazines. As Eugene Current-García points out, "no other American writer of stories had been so widely read, enjoyed, discussed, approved of, and imitated."[26] By 1920, nearly five million copies of his books had been sold in the United States alone.

Although the short story has always been popular in America, the English, with the exception of modern Irish writers, have never excelled in the form. The reason may have something to do with the English emphasis on a cohesive society: critic and literary historian Lionel Stevenson has suggested that as soon as a culture becomes more complex, brief narratives expand to reflect that social complexity.[27] As Frank O'Connor and other short story writers and critics have noted, the short story seems to thrive best in a fragmented society.[28] As Wendell Harris has noted, the fragmentation of sensibility necessary for the development of the short story did not begin in England until about 1880, at which time the form came to the fore as the best medium for presenting it. With this fragmentation, perspective or "angle of vision" becomes most important in the short story, which does not present a world to enter, as does the novel, but a vignette to contemplate. The essence of the short story, says Harris, "is to isolate, to portray the individual person, or moment, or scene in isolation—detached from the great continuum—at once social and historical. . . . The short story is indeed the natural vehicle for the presentation of the outsider, but also for the moment whose intensity makes it seem outside the ordinary stream of time . . . or outside our ordinary range of experience."[29]

The 1890s, the period that H. G. Wells called "the Golden Age" of the short story in England, derived, albeit in an indirect way, from Edgar Allan Poe; for it was Poe who inspired Baudelaire, who in turn inspired the symbolist movement, which ultimately gave impetus to the development of the short story during this period. The view that art should deemphasize the social and emphasize the formal dominated what critics have termed the "state of mind" that defined the 1890s in English literature. Short fiction of the so-called fin-de-siècle exemplifies this view in various ways, from the allegory of George Gissing's "House of Cobwebs" to the parable form of Arthur Symonds's "Christian Trevalga."

Because of the emphasis on aesthetic reality in the 1890s, it is no coincidence that the first British writer to be recognized as a specialist in the short story, Robert Louis Stevenson, was—like Ambrose Bierce in America—the champion of the romance form in the latter part of the nineteenth century. Nor is it a coincidence that he was one of the first British short fiction writers to focus—as did Henry James—on technique and form rather than on content alone. Like Bierce, Stevenson urged that literature, in its most typical mode of narrative, flees from external reality and pursues "an independent and creative aim." The work of art exists not by its resemblance to life, "but by its immeasurable difference from life," wrote Stevenson.[30] Both Lionel Stevenson and Walter Allen claim that the watershed for the modern short story began in 1878 with the publication of Stevenson's "A Lodging for the Night"; Allen goes so far as to insist that the change to the specifically modern short story can be precisely dated at that point.[31]

Although Stevenson was the first British writer to build his career on the short story form, it was Rudyard Kipling's short fiction that was the first to stimulate a great deal of criticism, much of it adverse. However, much of the negative criticism Kipling has received is precisely the same criticism that has often been lodged against the short story in general—for example, that the form focuses only on episodes, that it is too concerned with technique, that it is too dependent on tricks, and that it often lacks moral force. Lionel Trilling notes that the words "craft" and "craftily" are Kipling's favorites, and Edmund Wilson says that it is the paradox of his career that he "should have extended the conquests of his craftsmanship in proportion to the shrinking of the range of his dramatic imagination."[32]

Kipling's best-known stories—"The Man Who Would be King," "Without Benefit of Clergy," "Mary Postgate," and "The Gardener"—are perfect representations of the transition point between the old-fashioned tale of the nineteenth century and the modern short story. Yet it was not Kipling but Joseph Conrad who, because of the profundity of his vision and the subtlety of his use of language, effectively made the transition. Many critics have suggested that "The Man Who Would Be King" is one of Kipling's most Conrad-like stories; but they also lament that Kipling evades the metaphysical issues implicit in the story and refuses to venture on the great philosophic generalizations that Conrad explored.

Indeed, most critics agree that it is Conrad who pioneered the true modern tale with a narrative technique that looks backward to Poe and forward to Joyce. The basis of Conrad's symbolism/impressionism is his conviction, reminiscent of Poe, that fiction must aspire to the magic suggestiveness of music, and that explicitness is fatal to art. However, Conrad tried—where Joyce later succeeded, in such famous stories as "The Dead"—to convey this magical suggestiveness by focusing on concrete situations in the real world. In one of his most famous symbolist/impressionistic stories, "The Secret Sharer," he grounds the romantic theme of the psychological double in a character who exists both outside and inside the protagonist simultaneously. This creation of an "as-if-real" character to embody psychic processes marks the impressionistic extension of Poe's use of obsessive characters to embody such processes.

Chekhov, Mansfield, Joyce

After the innovations of Hawthorne, Poe, and Melville at midcentury, the second major shift in the development of the form was signaled by the "new" realism of Anton Chekhov. Chekhov's short stories were first welcomed in England and America just after the turn of the twentieth century as examples of late-nineteenth-century realism, but since they did not embody the social commitment or political convictions of the realistic novel; they were termed "realistic," rather, primarily because they seemed to focus on fragments of everyday reality—and so were character-ized as "sketches," "cross sections," or "slices of life." Even as they were widely noted as lacking the elements that constitute a really good short story, other critics saw that Chekhov's impressionism and his freedom from the literary conventions of the highly plot-ted and formalized story marked the beginnings of a new or "modern" kind of short fiction—one that combined the specific detail of realism with the poetic lyricism of romanticism.

Chekhov's conception of the short story as a lyrically charged fragment in which characters are less fully rounded figures of real-ism than embodiments of mood has influenced all twentieth-cen-tury practitioners of the form. Yet his most immediate impact was manifest in the work of the three writers active during the first two decades of this century who have received the most critical attention for fully developing the so-called modern short story—James Joyce, Katherine Mansfield, and Sherwood Anderson.

The most obvious similarity between the stories of Chekhov and those of Joyce, Anderson, and Mansfield is their minimal dependence on the traditional notion of plot. Like Chekhov, both Anderson and Joyce focus on the central themes of isola-tion, the need for human sympathy, and the moral failure of inaction, all of which dominate the modernist movement in the early twentieth century. Both forswear highly plotted stories in favor of seemingly static episodes and "slices" of reality. Both depend on unity of feeling to create a sense of "storyness." Both establish a sense of the seemingly casual out of that which is deliberately patterned, creating significance out of the trivial by judicious selection of detail and a meaningful ordering of the parts. The result is an objective-ironic style that has characterized the modern short story up to the present day.

Like Chekhov, whom she greatly admired, Katherine Mans-field was often accused of writing sketches instead of stories because her works were recognized as not manifesting the plot-ted action of nineteenth-century short fiction. The Mansfield story best known for its similarity in technique and theme to the typical Chekhov story is "The Fly," which, like "Misery," is about the nature of grief and which maintains a strictly objective point of view to communicate the latent significance of the protago-nist's emotional state.

Whereas the modern British short story began with the Russian influence of Chekhov, critics of the short story such as

H. E. Bates and Frank O'Connor have suggested that the modern Irish short story began with George Moore's publication of *The Untilled Field* in 1903. Others have concurred with Moore's own typically immodest assessment that the collection was a "frontier book, between the new and the old style" of fiction.[33] Moore's stories, by combining the content of French naturalism and the concern for style of the fin-de-siècle aesthetes, seem to be unique for their time. A basic tenet of Moore's aesthetic is that reality must be understood by means of narrative—a concept that can be clearly seen in his best-known and most-anthologized story, "Julia Cahill's Curse," which uses the folktale mode as a means of presenting, and understanding, social reality. Moore presents a story in both the old and the new way, that is, as a literal story of magic and as a symbolic story to account for the breakdown of the parish life.

Moore prepared the way for the innovative technique of James Joyce, who pushed the trivial and seemingly inconsequential realistic story to more subtle epiphanic extremes in *Dubliners*, the collection of short stories that marks the end of the nineteenth-century short fiction tradition in Anglo-Irish literature. Joyce's best-known story, "The Dead," clearly illustrates that, in short fiction, it is only the end of the story, when Gabriel accepts death, that unifies the preceding details and makes them thematically meaningful.

Sherwood Anderson to the Present

The shift that took place between the end of the nineteenth century and the rebirth of short fiction in America in the 1920s has been attributed largely to a loss of confidence in the authority of social reality. Bonaro Overstreet has suggested that nineteenth-century short stories depended on two basic faiths: that one can know right from wrong because a basic social code of values was taken for granted, and that people are what they seem to be. In the twentieth century, says Overstreet, perhaps as a result of World War I, these faiths were lost and, consequently, we are "thrown back upon a study of human nature—human motives, fears, wants, prejudices." The drama of the twentieth century, says Overstreet, is "the drama of what goes on in the mind." And the short story is an "expert medium for the expression of our deep concern about human moods and motives."[34]

An extensive study of these shifts and their many implications for short fiction of this period can be seen in Austin Wright's *The American Short Story in the Twenties*. Wright says that Anderson's, Hemingway's, and Faulkner's stories are better than are those of Mary Wilkins Freeman, Hamlin Garland, and William Dean Howells primarily because of the way they grapple with the loss of confidence in the adequacy of the social system and the new reliance on the individual self. Whereas nineteenth-century interest in moral problems focused on how to resolve the dilemma within the social system, Wright says, "in stories of the twenties, on the other hand, the more fully developed moral problems have no solution, and their interest centers more directly on the question of sympathy for the bewildered individual." While there was substantial agreement in the nineteenth century on the worth of society and social principles as moral guidance, says Wright, the world of the 1920s was "fragmented both socially and morally, with each man isolated, obliged to find or make for himself his appropriate place in society and the appropriate principles to guide him."[35] Sherwood Anderson's *Winesburg, Ohio* has often been cited by critics as the new century's groundbreaking collection of short stories that best embodies this point of view.

After the publication of *Winesburg, Ohio* in 1919, the short story in America flowered and flourished. The stories of Ernest Hemingway, influenced by Turgenev's combination of naturalism and lyricism and Joyce's epiphanic technique, pushed to further extremes the Chekhovian technique of communicating complex emotional states by the seemingly simple patterning of concrete detail. In such stories as "Big Two-Hearted River" and "Hills Like White Elephants," Chekhovian reticence reaches such extremes that all traditional notions of story seem to have disappeared for the sake of what Frank O'Connor has called the "artful approach to the significant moment."[36]

In the nearly forty years between the publication of *Winesburg, Ohio* and Bernard Malamud's 1958 National Book Award–winning *The Magic Barrel*, the "artful approach" initiated by Chekhov and Joyce came to dominate short fiction. The result, aided by the New Criticism's emphasis on the analysis of technique, was an increasingly formalist "literary story" that many critics complained merely constituted a new formula to replace the old trick-ending story

of O. Henry and his followers—a literary formula of the inconclusive incident and the unresolved impasse.

However, despite the "new realism" introduced by Chekhov,
Joyce, and Anderson early in the century, the short story still
retained its links to its older mythic and romance forms. Thus,
two strains of the short story developed in the first half of the
century: on the one hand, a stark new realistic style typified by
Hemingway and his Russian precursor Isaac Babel, and, on the
other, a more mythic style evinced by such writers as William
Faulkner, who created a mythic world in the American South,
and Isak Dinesen, who invented modern Gothic fairy tales. Both
styles merged lyricism with symbolism, and both were progres-
sively pushed to such extremes that what Malcolm Cowley
called Hemingway's "nightmares at noonday" ultimately developed into the more radically realized nightmares of Franz Kafka,
while the moral legends of Isak Dinesen evolved into the grotesque Gothic romances of Flannery O'Connor.[37]

Both styles are combined in the stories of Katherine Anne
Porter, Eudora Welty, John Steinbeck, Carson McCullers, John
Cheever, Richard Wright, Truman Capote, Isaac B. Singer, and
Bernard Malamud during this period. Though seemingly disparate, the work of these writers has much in common—most
notably, a focus on the grotesque, the use of traditional folktale
structures and motifs, a concern with aesthetic experience, an
obsession with dream experience, a search for style and form, an
insistence on the importance of language, the use of surrealistic
imagery, and the development of a tightly unified poetic form.

Both the differences and the similarities between the two
styles can be seen quite clearly in the stories of Isaac Babel and
Isak Dinesen. Babel takes a rather narrow spectrum of experience for his subject matter, but it is his focus on the revelatory
moment and his understanding of the short story as a form of
aesthetic contemplation that makes him a powerful force in
modern European short fiction. Similarly, Isak Dinesen, who
derives her stories from medieval legends and tales and deals
with life as an aesthetic game or a marionette theater, is primarily
interested in stories that are about storytelling itself.

Kafka's powerful place in modern European short fiction stems
from his ability to combine the primitive dream reality of Babel
and Dinesen with the complex aesthetic sophistication of such
writers as Thomas Mann and Vladimir Nabokov. Because his fic-

tions are so evasive, so complex in their admixture of the world of everyday reality and the world of nightmare and story, they lend themselves to a variety of critical approaches—formalist, Freudian, structuralist, and poststructuralist. Indeed, in Kafka's short stories one can find traces of virtually every convention of the European short fiction tradition—from the grotesque tragicomic style of Gogol to the intensified hyperreality of Chekhov, to the self-reflexive aesthetic games of Nabokov.

This increasing push to extremes of both the realistic and the mythic styles has continued up through the second half of the century: short story writers of the period between 1960 and 1990 can also be said, roughly, to fall into two different groups. On the one hand, the ultimate extreme of the mythic-romance is the fantastic antistory style of Jorge Luis Borges, Donald Barthelme, John Barth, and Robert Coover. On the other hand, the extremes of Chekhovian realism can be seen in the so-called "minimalism" of Ann Beattie, Mary Robison, Raymond Carver, and Tobias Wolff. The very fact that the mythic style of such writers as Gabriel García Márquez is sometimes called "magical realism," while the minimalist style of Raymond Carver is sometimes called "hyperrealism" indicates that the twin streams of romance and realism are inextricably blended in the works of contemporary short story writers.

However, as this survey and the following chapters attempt to illustrate, the development of the short story as a literary genre has always been characterized by a tension between the traditional mythic origins of the form and the increasing pressures of modernism to depict "real life." When this tension is combined with the intrinsic demands of the very shortness of the form—to present either an illustrative anecdote that embodies timeless truth, or to focus on a moment of time that meaningfully breaks up the routine of everyday reality—the result is a narrative form that demonstrates a high degree of artistic stylization yet has always remained close to what the Cardinal in Isak Dinesen's "The Cardinal's First Tale" calls the "divine art of story." "In the beginning was the story" says the Cardinal, and within our whole universe, "the story only has authority to answer that cry of heart of its characters, that one cry of heart of each of them: *'Who am I?'"*[38]

Chapter 2

NINETEENTH-CENTURY BEGINNINGS

Although most critics and literary historians agree that short fiction underwent a change in the mid-nineteenth century, especially in America, the nature of that change has never been made clear. Certainly, short narratives existed before the period between 1820 and 1860, during which Washington Irving, Nathaniel Hawthorne, Edgar Allan Poe, and Herman Melville irrevocably transformed the short story. However, earlier short fiction forms, such as folktales, short romances, fables, and ballads were for the most part allegorically code-bound rather than realistically mimetic. These were highly formalized genres, either controlled by an inherited traditional story or illustrative of an abstract idea. Short fiction *prior to* the nineteenth century was not determined by the use of specific detail and real-time events to provide a verisimilar version of the everyday world, as was the longer fiction of the eighteenth century. Yet, because early nineteenth-century short-fiction writers were descendants of an era in which reality was ascribed to concrete particulars, they could neither ignore the increasingly realistic techniques of Defoe, Richardson, and Fielding nor accept the supernaturalism that formed the basis of the older, allegorical short forms. By combining the code-bound narrative conventions of the old allegorical romance forms with the verisimilar techniques of the new mimetic forms, they created a new genre that would later in the century be called the "short story."

The difference between long and short fiction correlates with—and very likely derives from—two contrasting assumptions about the nature of reality. If reality consists of human interaction with the physical and social world in time, then the best way to reflect that reality is to create a similitude of the physical and social world by means of specific, time-bound detail. If, on the other hand, reality is primarily a transcendent, timeless ideal or a projection of human desire for transcendence, the best way to reflect it is to construct narratives that center on revelatory moments when that ideal or desire is manifested.

The short story, which tends to express the second assumption, is primarily a romantic rather than a realistic form, in which revelation—what the romantic poets described with phrases such as "moments of vision"—reflects true reality. Like the old romance form, the short story focuses on the sacred rather than the profane, the universal rather than the particular. Yet it differs fundamentally from the old romance in that the revelatory moment is experienced by an individual perceiver; it is not the result of the direct intervention of an absolute, transcendent reality. The consequence of this mix of romanticism and reality for long fiction in the nineteenth century was the hybrid genre now called the "modern romance"—which is best represented by Emily Brontë's *Wuthering Heights* but is also reflected in the novels of the two most widely read authors of the period, Charles Dickens and Thomas Hardy, who created characters that seemed both real and conventional at the same time.

European Origins

In Germany, in the first quarter of the nineteenth century, the *novella* began to detach itself from the comic satire and moral exemplum inspired by Boccaccio and Cervantes, and even to be supported by a theory of its own. Friedrich von Schlegel agreed with the Renaissance idea that a *novella* was an anecdote that must be capable of arousing interest, but he noted, further, that the modern retelling of already-known traditional stories necessarily focuses the reader's attention away from mythic authority and toward the authority of the narrator's subjective viewpoint. This grounding of the mythic in the psychological is most clearly seen in E. T. A. Hoffmann, whose stories are often self-conscious manipulations of the relationship between fantasy and the everyday.

Modern Russian short fiction, of course, begins with Nikolai Gogol, whose major stylistic innovation was the combining of the fanciful and earthy folklore of his native Ukraine with the literary and philosophic imagination of the German Romanticism he had learned in school. Gogol's combination of fantastic events with realistic detail reaches a powerful culmination when he unites it with two different literary styles in what virtually every critic agrees is his most nearly perfect work, "The Overcoat." The story of the poverty-stricken little copyist with the absurd name of Akaky Akakievich has been so influential that it has been said that all modern Russian fiction springs from under Gogol's "Overcoat."

The secret of the success of "The Overcoat" is Gogol's combination of social realism reflective of everyday Petersburg life with the fantastic style of folklore. Irish short story writer Frank O'Connor has said that what makes the story so magnificent is Gogol's focus on the little man and his emphasis on Akaky's implicit call for human brotherhood.[1] On the other hand, in what is perhaps the best-known analysis of the story, Russian formalist critic B. M. Éjxenbaum claims that the genius of "The Overcoat" depends on the role played by the author's personal tone and the story's use of the oral conventions of the Russian folktale.[2] From his nineteenth-century countryman Ivan Turgenev to the twentieth-century American philosopher and fiction writer William H. Gass, Gogol has been recognized as a powerful innovator in the development of that strange blend of fantasy and reality—the comic grotesque—we have come to recognize as an essential element of modernism and postmodernism.

The first work of short fiction in English literature to experiment with such a combination of the old romance and the new realism, a work that set the tone for much nineteenth-century English and American short fiction to follow, is Horace Walpole's

23

"The Castle of Otranto," published in 1765. In the famous preface to the second edition, Walpole says his work is an attempt to blend two kinds of romance, the ancient and the modern. "In the former, all was imagination and improbability: in the latter, nature is intended to be, and sometimes has been, copied with success." Noting that "fancy" had been dammed up by an adherence to common life in the modern romance, where in the ancient romance, nature or reality was excluded, Walpole characterized his reconciliation task as follows: "Desirous of leaving the powers of fancy at liberty to expatiate through the boundless realms of invention, and thence of creating more interesting situations," Walpole noted he wished to construct "the mortal agents in his drama according to the rules of probability: in short, to make them think, speak, and act, as it might be supposed mere men and women do in extraordinary positions."[3]

Washington Irving

In spite of these initial experiments in Europe, short fiction's combination of the romantic and the realistic begins most vigorously in the United States. The reason was primarily economic: American writers stood little chance of competing against English novelists, whose works were cheaply and readily available in America because of the lack of copyright control. The American periodical magazine form, the perfect vehicle for short fiction, thus arose in part to provide a means for American writers to publish their work. However, American writers faced still another problem: how could they make use of existing generic forms such as allegory, Gothic romance, the novel, and the eighteenth-century narrative essay, and yet create something that was truly their own?

Washington Irving solved this problem by grounding traditional German folktales in American settings and by providing these legends with a sophisticated eighteenth-century teller. Thus, in "The Legend of Sleepy Hollow" and "Rip Van Winkle," he was able to depict an American cultural conflict between the sleepy old Dutch world of the early settlers and the hustle and bustle of Yankee capitalism and democracy. The defeat and dismissal of Ichabod Crane, the acquisitive Yankee who wished to take over the old Dutch world, is romantic wish-fulfillment, for his spirit still dominates American life, while the old world persists only as imaginative ghosts in the minds of children. Similarly, Rip Van Winkle sleeps for twenty-five years, moving from childhood to second childhood without the intervening annoyance of adulthood, and awakening to the new world of American society as an aged man who preserves the old world the only way it can be preserved—in the imaginative realm of stories. Irving's use of a sophisticated localized teller displaces his stories from their legendary roots toward social reality and satire without losing their sense of idealized and projective dream reality.

Although Irving is the first American writer to popularize short fiction in America, it is Hawthorne, Poe, and Melville who combine the conventions of medieval allegorical romance, eighteenth-century realism, and the nineteenth-century Gothic in a complex way that results in a new narrative form that later becomes known as the short story. To illustrate how these writers achieved this blending of old genres to create a new one, I will discuss three of their best-known stories: Hawthorne's "Young Goodman Brown," Poe's "The Fall of the House of Usher," and Melville's "Bartleby the Scrivener."

Nathaniel Hawthorne

The problem faced by both Poe and Hawthorne in making use of the old allegorical and Gothic romance forms was how to give them the verisimilitude of the more realistic fiction of the time and still maintain the strong sense of formal unity and symbolic significance typical of the old allegorical and romance forms. Whereas the demand for realism did not allow Hawthorne and Poe to rely on the preestablished unity of received story or abstract truth that underlay the old forms, both admitted they were unable by tradition or individual talent to write entirely realistic social fiction.

Hawthorne experimented with combining the eighteenth-century essay with the legendary or allegorical story, as did Irving before him, writing a number of sketches that had some of the loose Addison and Steele discursiveness about them but that symbolically suggested a universal moral truth. "Wakefield" is perhaps the prototypical example of how Hawthorne combined medieval allegory and the eighteenth-century essay to create a "real-life" situation with symbolic significance. The basic problem the narrator in "Wakefield" faces in telling this story about a man who left his wife for twenty years with no explanation is of course to provide that missing explanation. To invent a realistic motivation, an explanation that has the merits of plausibility, though—for example, that Wakefield left because of his love for another woman, or that he could no longer stand living with his wife—would have been to write a "slice of life" story of everyday reality. Hawthorne is drawn to the case of Wakefield, however, precisely because of its mystery and its disruption of everyday reality. He imagines that although Wakefield must have taken this "singular step with the consciousness of a purpose," he cannot "define it sufficiently for his own contemplation."

Hawthorne's narrator's explanation of the act, typical of the old allegorical forms, is general rather than specific. He imagines the reason for Wakefield's initial gesture is vanity, the perverse need to create a reaction; thus, he paradoxically focuses attention on the self by absenting self. Hawthorne says that if he were writing a long book, he might be able to explain how an influence beyond human control "lays its strong hand on every deed which we do, and weaves its consequences into an iron tissue of necessity." Since he is writing only a short "article," he simply asserts that Wakefield becomes frozen in his own gesture.

Many of Poe's stories are also experiments with combining narrative with the eighteenth-century essay conventions; however, instead of combining essay with allegory, as Hawthorne does, Poe transforms the objective essay viewpoint into the confession of an obsessed narrator-protagonist. "The Imp of the Perverse" is a clear example of this combination, similar to "Wakefield" in that the central gesture in the story is an act that cannot be explained realistically or psychologically. The story begins with an essay format with a description of the human propensity Poe calls a "*prima mobilia*" of the soul—"an innate and primitive principle of human action, a paradoxical something, which we may call *perverseness*, for want of a more characteristic term."

Having discussed the perverse as the ultimate motiveless obsession and even given examples of it, the objective and distanced essayist of "The Imp of the Perverse" becomes an obsessed and involved narrator who philosophizes about perverse motiveless motive as a way to justify his own behavior. It is not the narrator's wrongdoing that results from perverseness, but rather his confession. After four years of not being suspected of murder, he feels safe; however, it is precisely his uttering the phrase "I am safe" that begins to undermine him. Knowing that he is safe if only he does not confess, he feels compelled by this very suggestion to confess. Perverseness, for Poe, is a fascinating paradox, because it is unreasonable precisely in proportion to the fact that reason urges it.

Hawthorne's most famous and most discussed story, "Young Goodman Brown," manifests the combination of the conventions of the old allegorical form and new realistic narrative by its central ambiguity. The controversy that has generated several hundred articles and book chapters on "Young Goodman Brown" derives primarily from Hawthorne's querying the reader near the end of the story: "Had Goodman Brown fallen asleep in the forest and only dreamed a wild dream of a witch-meeting?" Numerous critics have tried to answer this question according to a variety of ideological and theoretical frameworks. I would contend that because Hawthorne was attempting to combine an allegorical form with a realistic one, the result is an inevitable ambiguity about the ontological, and therefore generic, status of the characters and the events in the story.

Hawthorne's problem in "Young Goodman Brown" is how to make the transition from a code-bound allegorical narrative to psychological verisimilitude without sacrificing the sense of an underlying moral meaning and the tight formal unity of such allegorical narratives. He achieves this in two different ways: first, by creating a protagonist who, even though he is a code-bound allegorical figure, seems to be at the same time an individual social character with his own consciousness; and second, by establishing a skeptical point of view that undercuts the supernatural authority of the legendary tale.

On the one hand, the story seems allegorical in that Goodman Brown is ritualistically predestined to enter the forest on this "one night" of "all nights in the year." On the other hand, the story seems realistic in that he consciously questions the journey and acts as if he could struggle against it. Since there is

no realistic motivation for his journey into the forest, no indication that it is a social custom for everyone in the village to make
this journey in his or her turn, the "cause" of the journey must
be ritual or legend: Brown's journey is motivated by the nature
of the underlying allegorical abstraction from which this particular story derives.

Brown does not act as an allegorical figure would, though, but
rather as a realistic character who is caught in an allegorical
structure of which he seems intermittently aware. For example,
he has "scruples" about his "present evil purpose" in the forest,
and he even considers turning back. A purely allegorical figure
cannot challenge the code-bound structure of the allegory itself;
he can only follow its preestablished demands. Moreover, the
facts that the devil resembles Brown, and that his words seem to
spring from Brown himself, suggest that Brown is a realistic figure able to create such a mental projection of the self, not an allegorical projection created by tradition or the author.

Hawthorne's tactical blending of allegory and realism in
"Young Goodman Brown" turns for the most part on the most
emphatic allegorical reference in the story—the name of Faith.
The narrator tells us that she is "aptly named," which suggests
both that she has the realistic quality of being faithful, and that
she is an allegorical embodiment of Brown's own faith. Each time
her name is used signals a crucial turning point in the story's status as either allegory or realism, or both. When Brown makes a
conscious decision and cries out, "With heaven above and Faith
below, I will stand firm against the devil," he hears Faith's voice
in the forest and changes his mind. When he cries out, "Faith!"
and the forest echoes him, her ribbon comes floating down, and
he feels lost. When he cries, "My Faith is gone. . . . There is no
good on earth; and sin is but a name," he begins his mad dash
through the forest to fulfill his destiny at the witches' sabbath.
Finally, when he speaks to Faith directly, telling her to look up to
heaven and resist the wicked one, the allegorical realm of the
story comes to a close, and Brown returns once more to everyday
reality.

Hawthorne's use of the skeptical eighteenth-century narrator
serves, in a similar way, to make the generic status of the story
ambiguous by questioning the supernatural authority of the
events. It is a common eighteenth- and nineteenth-century

device of narrative verisimilitude to validate the authority and truth of story by establishing its legendary or mythic source. However, Hawthorne's narrator does not say that the story of Goodman Brown has been handed down to him from previous generations, that it was told to him by someone of authority, or that it is something he read in an authoritative book.

This refusal to provide an authentic source for the tale allows the narrator to adopt a skeptical tone whereby even as he relates the fantastic events as truth he undercuts their probability. For example, when he describes the stranger's staff turning into a great black snake, he undermines this by noting that it "must have been an ocular deception, assisted by the uncertain light." When he describes Goody Cloyse mumbling some indistinct words, he notes parenthetically "a prayer, doubtless." The central skeptical challenge to the events, of course, comes when Goodman Brown returns to the village and Faith comes out joyfully to meet him. When he passes her by without a greeting, the narrator wonders: "Had Goodman Brown fallen asleep in the forest and only dreamed a wild dream of a witch-meeting?"

This query raises a significant problem regarding the genre of the story. If we are to take the event in the forest as having actually happened, it is too extreme to be true except as an allegorical occurrence; however, if Goodman Brown dreamed it, then he is an individual consciousness capable of dreaming. The problem with "Young Goodman Brown" is that it seems to be both allegory and dream—as if a realistic character had entered an allegorical reality so fantastic that there could be no explanation for it except that it is a dream. "Young Goodman Brown" may be the fulfillment of Hawthorne's stated desire "to write a dream which shall resemble the real course of a dream, with all its inconsistency, its strange transformations, which are all taken as a matter of course; its eccentricities and aimlessness—with nevertheless a leading idea running through the whole." As the Custom House sketch in *The Scarlet Letter* clearly indicates, Hawthorne was well aware of that "neutral territory, somewhere between the real world and fairyland, where the Actual and the Imaginary may meet, and each imbue itself with the nature of the other."

Using short fiction to present a universal abstract truth as if it were the psychic projection of a single individual inevitably shifts a story's emphasis from reality understood as a result of supernatural or social forces to reality understood as a function of the secret psyche of the individual. This basically romantic apprehension of reality largely accounts for Frank O'Connor's well-known intuition that we find in the short story "at its most characteristic something we do not often find in the novel—an intense awareness of human loneliness".[4] "Young Goodman Brown" reflects a common theme in the short story that persists up to the present: although social or public reality is inauthentic, the true reality of the secret private life is always ambiguous.[5]

The people that Brown sees at the witches' gathering are those he has seen in public life and has thought to exemplify innocence, dignity, or holiness—characters, that is, who are the sum total of their social personae. What he discovers is that human reality is more complex and problematic than social inter-action reveals, indeed, that true human reality is often at odds with everyday social reality. He and Faith are welcomed as initi-ates to that true reality. "Welcome, my children . . . to the com-munion of your race. Ye have found thus young your nature and your destiny." They are told that they are to be initiated into the "mystery of sin," conscious of the "secret guilt" of others, and that since evil is the nature of mankind, evil must be their only happiness.

The problem with this "language of the devil" in the story is that Hawthorne does not make it clear what the nature of "evil" or "sin" is. Many critics have interpreted these statements literal-ly, as indications either of Hawthorne's pessimism or Goodman Brown's Calvinism. However, since it is not realistically plausible that everyone in the town is evil or sinful or that they are all liter-al followers of the devil, the words "evil" and "sin" here must be understood in a more general way than merely signifying specif-ic wrongdoing. If we are to take "Young Goodman Brown" as an initiation story about the discovery of evil, as many critics do, then it might be well to compare it to that archetypal story of the discovery of evil in the book of Genesis.

Erich Fromm, in his study *The Art of Loving*, makes helpful suggestions about how to understand the Garden of Eden story. The first effect of Adam and Eve's eating of the forbidden fruit is that they look at each other and are ashamed. Fromm says the shame has a deeper meaning than merely to signify the birth of sexual prudery. The eating of the apple marks the separation of one entity into two separate entities, who must henceforth be condemned to loneliness and isolation.[5] *This* is the true nature of the universal "sin" of human reality that Goodman Brown discovers.

According to the Christian religion, the only way to heal this separation is to follow the commandment of Jesus to love one's neighbor as oneself. However, as Fromm reminds us, this suggests not a narrow egotism but rather that we love the neighbor until we can make no distinction between the neighbor and the self. Before his journey into the forest, Goodman Brown simply assumed the sense of union, as children do; the journey into the forest is a metaphor for his discovery that separation and isolation—the unknowable and unsayable secret of everyone's inner psychic life—is the nature of humanity. Once he has made this discovery, Goodman Brown has only two choices: he can accept the truth of separation and engage in the noble fiction of loving the other as a means to heal it or he can fall into despair and hopelessness. In "Young Goodman Brown," Faith, "aptly named," is able to make the leap of faith and hold out her arms in love. Goodman Brown, however, cannot; thus, he goes to his grave an emblem of isolation and despair.

By combining the code-bound conventions of allegory and romance with the contextually based realistic conventions of the novel, Hawthorne creates a story that has both the unity of allegory, held together by a powerful idea and an overall intentional pattern, and the hallucinatory effect of dream reality, made realistic by psychological plausibility and the specificity of concrete detail—all elements of short fiction that have persisted up to the present day.

Edgar Allan Poe

Many of the critical controversies over Poe's "The Fall of the House of Usher" and Melville's "Bartleby the Scrivener" have arisen from the stories' generic mix of the conventions of romance and realism. Although our basic question about both Usher and Bartleby is "What is the *matter* with them?" they have no *matter*. To ask what is the "matter" with them is to encounter the same frustration that Shakespeare's Gertrude faces when she asks Polonius to give her "more matter, less art," and that Polonius himself feels when Hamlet tells him he is reading "words, words, words" and Polonius insists, "I mean, what is the matter?" For there is no matter to Usher or Bartleby, only art. Both are primarily code-bound functions of the story they inhabit, even as they seem to inhabit the world of everyday reality.

The narrators in both stories *are*, on the other hand, "as-if-real" characters who, like the readers they reflect, have difficulty understanding Usher and Bartleby when they apply their own realistic standards to them. The narrator in Poe's story says he cannot connect Usher's expression with any idea of simple humanity, while Melville's lawyer says there is nothing ordinarily human about Bartleby. Poe's narrator continually reiterates his puzzlement and his failure to understand Usher, while Melville's narrator continually tries to get Bartleby to follow the rules of common sense and common usage.

What makes "The Fall of the House of Usher" a unified and meaningful tale, rather than merely a Gothic potboiler, is Poe's romantic conviction that true reality is neither physical nor social but, rather, aesthetic. The story begins with the entrance of the narrator into the world of Usher, which is the world of the story itself. The landscape that surrounds the house—the "rank sedges," "the white trunks of decayed trees," the "singularly dreary tract of country"—are archetypal images found in Turgenev's "Bezhin Meadow," Conrad's "Heart of Darkness," Sherwood Anderson's "The Man Who Became a Woman," and many other short stories. It is a landscape that, like the wasteland of Robert Browning's "Childe Roland to the Dark Tower Came," objectifies a nightmarish psychic world cut off from ordinary everyday reality.

It is the house itself, however—because it is both an objective reality and a literary metaphor—that creates interpretative difficulties for the narrator: "I know not how it was—but, with the first glimpse of the building, a sense of insufferable gloom pervaded my spirit." He justifies this feeling as insufferable because it is not relieved by the poetic sentiment that usually allows one to accept the sternest natural images of the desolate and terrible. Furthermore, he says the house creates such a sense of "unredeemed dreariness of thought" that no "goading of the imagination could torture into aught of the sublime." He himself poses the basic interpretative question about the house and thus the story: "What was it that so unnerved me in the contemplation of the House of Usher? It was a mystery all insoluble".[7]

The narrator knows that although certain combinations of natural objects have the power of affecting one in such a way, the "analysis of this power lies among considerations beyond our depth." Thinking that perhaps a "different arrangement of the particulars of the scene, of the details of the picture, would be sufficient to modify, or perhaps to annihilate its capacity for sorrowful impression," he tries the experiment of looking at the house from the perspective of its reflection in the tarn ("Usher," 231). However, the inverted reflected image, much like a distorted image in one of Poe's own stories, makes him shudder more than the house itself did. In this highly stylized opening, the narrator simulates the process by which the reader enters into the patterned reality of the artwork, obviously affected but puzzled as to what could have created such an effect.

Like other unitary Poe figures, Roderick Usher is a character so identified with his single obsession that he has become a metaphoric embodiment of that obsession. Usher's fear is of no particular thing, as indeed it could not be, for it is the fear of ultimate nothingness. He says he dreads events of the future, not in themselves, but in their results—"in terror"—and he knows he must soon "abandon life and reason together, in some struggle with the grim phantasm, FEAR" ("Usher," 235). Usher's fear is not a plausible psychological fear but a fear that can be understood only in aesthetic terms. His "morbid acuteness of the senses"—which makes all but the most bland food intolerable, garments of anything but certain textures unwearable, the sight of anything but the faintest light unbearable, and all sounds except those from stringed instruments unendurable— means that Roderick Usher is the ultimate romantic artist, one who can no longer tolerate any sensory input at all and has cut himself from any stimulus from the external world.

Although we know little about Roderick as an "as-if-real" character, we do know that he is an artist who paints, improvises on the guitar, and writes poetry. And what characterizes his artistic works is what the narrator calls a "highly distempered ideality" that throws a "sulphurous lustre over all." Of his paintings, the narrator says, "if ever mortal painted an idea, that mortal was Roderick Usher" ("Usher," 237). Concerned only with the purest of abstraction, with no relation to objects in the world, Roderick's paintings are hermetically sealed: the one painting that the narrator does describe depicts a rectangular vault or tunnel under the earth, which has no outlet and no artificial light yet is nevertheless bathed in intense rays.

The underlying obsession of the story that so haunts Roderick is his conviction of the "sentience of vegetable things." He pushes this belief to an extreme in his theory of the "kingdom of inorganization," that is, the sentience of the structure of nonliving things, specifically the house itself: "The conditions of the sentience had been here, he imagined, fulfilled in the method of collocation of these stones—in the order of their arrangement, as well as in that of the many *fungi* which overspread them, and the decayed trees which stood around—above all in the long undisturbed endurance of this arrangement, and in its reduplication in the still waters of the tarn" ("Usher," 239).

This passage, a crucial statement about aesthetic pattern as the source of life, reminds us that since Roderick has cut himself off from any external sensory source for his art, all that he has left to feed on is himself; the only end possible for him is that he be swallowed up by the aesthetic world Poe creates. Near the end of the story, when the narrator reads to Roderick a romance entitled the "Mad Trist," sounds described in the story being read are echoed in the fictional world of Roderick and the narrator. The shriek of the dragon in the "Mad Trist" is echoed by a shriek in "The Fall of the House of Usher," as is the terrible ringing sound of the romance hero's shield. This is what Jean Ricardou has called the *mise en abyme* in the story— that point in which it refers self-reflexively to its own structure.[8]

This meshing of fiction and reality is what brings the story to its climax as Roderick shouts, "*Madman! I tell you that she now stands without the door!*" and the utterance has the "potency of a spell; the doors swing open and Madeline, Usher's sister, falls inward upon him with a moaning cry; like collapsing cards, he falls to the floor, and the house falls into the tarn. Everything collapses back into unformulated precreation nothingness, and the tale ends on the italicized words of its own title. In "The Fall of the House of Usher," Roderick is the ultimate romantic artist who desires to cut himself off from external reality and to live within the realm of pure imagination, although he fears the loss of self such an ultimate gesture inevitably entails. His belief that the house is sentient because of the particular organization of its parts is a metaphor for Poe's pushing the romantic aesthetic of organic unity to its ultimate extremes.

Herman Melville

In contrast, Melville's "Bartleby the Scrivener" presents not a realistic character entering into the aesthetic realm of imaginative reality, as does "Usher," but the reverse—an obsessed aesthetic figure invades the realm of everyday reality, realistically represented by the practical and prudent world of the law office on Wall Street. In the prologue to the story, the narrator says that where he might write the complete life of other scriveners, no "materials exist for a full and satisfactory biography of this man."[9] This is so because Bartleby is a metaphoric figure rather than a realistic one. The process underlying the narrator's dilemma has been explained well, though in another context, by Roman Jakobson, with his distinction between metaphoric and metonymic processes. Jakobson notes that whereas it is well known that the metaphoric process (in which an object stands for something else) forms the basis of romanticism and symbolism, it is less acknowledged that it is the predominance of metonymy (in which an object stands next to something else) that forms the basis of the realistic style. "Following the path of contiguous relationships, the realistic author metonymically digresses from the plot to the atmosphere and from the characters to the setting in space and time."[10] However, Bartleby has no setting in space or in time; in fact, he has no particular concrete social context at all.

Elizabeth Hardwick—who notes that out of the story's sixteen thousand words, Bartleby speaks only thirty-seven short lines, more than a third of which are "I would prefer not to"—describes the problem of Bartleby's character in the following way:

Bartleby's language reveals the all of him, but what is revealed? Character? Bartleby is not a character in the manner of the usual, imaginative, fictional construction. And he is not a character as we know them in life, with that bundling bustle of details, their suits and ties and felt hats, their love affairs surreptitious or binding, family albums, psychological justifications dragging like a little wagon along the highway of experience. . . . Bartleby has no plot in his present existence, and we would not wish to imagine subplots for his already lived years. He is indeed only words, wonderful words, and very few of them.[11]

Bartleby's statement "I am not particular" refers to his status as a fictional character derived from the tradition of the old romance: although he seems in some ways to be a particular character inhabiting the real world—for example, his seeming change from feverish copying to no copying at all—his actions also seem to be more predetermined than consciously decided upon. He seems to embody a "general" rather than a "particular" response to the universe. Melville must have taken sardonic delight in his metaphoric postscript at the end of the story, for to suggest that the "cause" of Bartleby's behavior is his previous job in a Dead Letter Office is merely to provide a placebo to the reader who, like the narrator himself, thirsts for logical or psychological explanations for everything. The postscript provides an answer that is no answer at all, except a purely metaphoric one. To create a character metonymically, the author must provide him or her with a concrete physical and social context—but Bartleby has *no* such context. His existence springs from his metaphoric mistake of reacting to the "dead letter" metaphor as if it were reality. Bartleby is not an "irreparable loss to literature," as the narrator suggests at the beginning of the story; rather, his existence is *solely* literary.

The fact that the only context we have for Bartleby is a metaphoric one is also suggested at the very beginning of the story, when the narrator says that a description of himself, his employees, his business, his chambers, and his general surroundings "is indispensable to an adequate understanding of the chief character about to be presented" ("Bartleby," 3). However, this context in which Bartleby is placed can be helpful in understanding Bartleby only in a metaphoric way. For example, what we know about the narrator himself is that he lives a "safe," "snug," "prudent," "methodical" existence. It is a romantic convention of short fiction, from Horace Walpole to Flannery O'Connor, that such snug smugness must be challenged by a mysterious stranger from the outside, a stranger whose reality is more metaphoric than metonymic.

We next learn about the surroundings of his chambers. Instead of finding the social or economic context of Wall Street, however, we are given only descriptions of the walls at each end of the narrator's chambers. Robert Marler says that one basic difference between the tale and the short story is that whereas in a tale such as "The Fall of the House of Usher" the wall with its crack is a symbol of Usher's madness, with little connection to the mundane world, in "Bartleby" the walls provide enclosures and support buildings, becoming symbolic only gradually through an accretion of meaning.[12] However, the very fact that Melville uses literal walls, which Bartleby transforms into metaphoric walls by his dead-wall reverie, should convince us sufficiently that the only function of the walls in this story—the walls of Wall Street, the walls of the Tombs, the wall in front of which Bartleby curls up in a fetal position and dies, the symbolic wall of the Dead Letter Office that stops efforts at communication—is to embody metaphorically Bartleby's existential realization of cosmic meaninglessness and human isolation.

The most striking aspect of the characters Turkey, Nippers, and Ginger Nut is their Dickensian grotesqueness and their metaphoric human emptiness. Neither Turkey or Nippers are whole in themselves, but taken together, like some mechanical creature out of a tale by E. T. A. Hoffman, they constitute one passably whole man. For the twelve-year-old Ginger Nut, the complexity of the law is metaphorically contained in a nutshell. None of these three characters is complex or whole enough to react meaningfully to the mystery of Bartleby. Whereas they are characterized in the Dickensian fashion of being little more than the sum of their idiosyncrasies, Bartleby metaphorically "stands for" a universal human awareness.

The ambiguous mixture of fabulistic figures and realistic detail in "Bartleby" has long been noted by critics. Newton Arvin has said that in no other writing did Melville achieve, "by the accumulation of details in themselves commonplace, prosaic, and humdrum, a total effect of such strangeness and even madness as this." The setting of "Bartleby," says Arvin, is not so much Wall Street offices as the "cosmic madhouse."[13] Robert Marler argues that "Bartleby"—as opposed to the romantic "tales" of Hawthorne and Poe—is the first fully developed "short story," because it is firmly embedded in a social context. However, Marler claims that, in keeping with the romantic spirit of previous short fiction, although "Bartleby" does reject supernaturalism and symbols not primarily functional in the story's natural order, its relative shortness conspires to force meaning beneath the surface—where, because of its indistinctness, it gives the impression of being inexplicable.[14]

"Bartleby" is problematic because it marks a transition between romance narratives, in which characters are two-dimensional representations, and realistic stories, in which they are presented as if they were real. The story seems so firmly grounded in social reality that it is difficult to take Bartleby as a purely symbolic character; at the same time, if we take him to be an "as-if-real" character, we have difficulty understanding what motivates him to act in the perverse way he does. We want to ask Bartleby, "What is the matter with you?" but we gradually begin to realize that he has no matter—which is to say, he can only react as a two-dimensional representation of passive rebellion. The one place in the story when he comes close to answering this question is when he has decided to do no more copying at all and the narrator asks him why. Bartleby, looking out the window at the blank wall, says, "Can you not see the reason for yourself?" ("Bartleby," 25).

The narrator, an "as-if-real" character, thinks there must be something wrong with Bartleby's eyes. Bartleby, however, is referring to the metaphoric motivation for his code-bound actions—the blank wall. Yet to tell an "as-if-real" person that the reason one has decided to do nothing is because of a wall is to invite suspicions of madness, for it means that Bartleby has taken a mere object in the world (the wall) to be that for which it stands (meaninglessness, nothingness, blankness, loneliness, isolation).

The narrator's sense that what he has seen in his office on Sunday morning makes him unfit for going to church suggests that he realizes the impossibility of obeying Christ's command to love his neighbor as himself. Although at the end of his patience with Bartleby the narrator asks what "earthly" right Bartleby has to stay there, what he tacitly understands is that because there is nothing "ordinarily human" about him, Bartleby has no "earthly" right; he has only the "heavenly" right urged by the divine injunction that the narrator remembers: "A new commandment give I unto you, that ye love one another" ("Bartleby," 30).

Although the narrator cannot identify with Bartleby's metaphoric mistake, he feels the power of Bartleby's loneliness and need. He knows that the only cure for Bartleby's isolation is brotherly love, but he is unable to grant that love on Bartleby's terms—that is, that he completely lose himself; what the metaphoric character Bartleby demands is nothing less than everything. However, because the "as-if-real" character feels he must exist in the practical everyday world, he ultimately must reject this spiritual demand. Although the narrator has intuitions about who or what Bartleby is, he cannot go all the way into that realm of madness, the metaphoric, and the sacred, that Bartleby inhabits; he can only tell the story over and over, each time trying to understand.

The narrator's looking into Jonathan Edwards on the "Will" and Joseph Priestly on "Necessity" is part of his effort to "account" for Bartleby. He begins to think that Bartleby has been placed with him for some "mysterious propose of an all-wise Providence, which it was not for a mere mortal like me to fathom" ("Bartleby," 31). And indeed, the problem Melville deals with here is the problem of the nature of necessity in fiction, for indeed things in fiction are predestinate, and the all-wise providence of any story is a combination of the author's individual talent and the tradition within which he or she works.

Bartleby and Usher ask their narrators to understand them, and the narrators, in telling their stories, ask the reader to understand why they did not understand them. Although the events in each story focus on narrators trying to understand aesthetic figures by the logic of the everyday, the discourse constructed by each of the narrators presents the figures in the only possible way to understand them—by rhetorical structure and metaphor. What is "realistic" about such short stories as "The Fall of the House of Usher" and "Bartleby" is what Erich Heller says is new about nineteenth-century realism generally—"the passion for understanding, the desire for rational appropriation, the driving force toward the expropriation of the mystery."[15] These two stories are dramatizations of just that effort at appropriation.

In the older, pre-nineteenth-century romance form, character was clearly a function of plot, and plot itself was a symbol of the psychological, metaphysical, and moral mysteries of universal human experience. With the rise of realism and the resultant focus on specific everyday experiences, the short story shifted from a symbolic embodiment of human experience to an illustrative example: instead of saying, with the authority of the old romance, "this is what human experience is," realistic fiction says, "given the way human experience is, this is what might happen." Whereas the old romance story says, "this is the way people are," the new realistic story says, "this is the way people act."

The basic limitation of realism, however, is that showing how people act does not in itself allow universal patterns of human experience to emerge. Realism, rather, gives the illusion that characters have a choice, that they might do one thing rather than another. However, such characters as Young Goodman Brown, Roderick Usher, and Bartleby seem somehow bound, obsessed, driven, and determined—even as the reader implicitly thinks that they "might" do something else if only they would turn back, get out, or snap out of it. No theologian can save Goodman Brown, no psychologist can cure Roderick Usher, and no meaningful job with good pay and social benefits can help Bartleby.

These three central characters in the nineteenth-century short story do not seem to be allegorical characters in the sense of the old romance form, yet they seem somehow caught in the conventions of allegory. Hawthorne achieves this effect by making the ontological status of Brown's world ambiguous: never clarifying whether his experience is dream or reality is much the same as never establishing clearly that what we are reading is allegory or actuality. Thus, the very mythic, traditional pattern of the story of the archetypal journey into the "heart of darkness" transforms an "as-if-real" character into an allegorical figure. In "The Fall of the House of Usher" and "Bartleby the Scrivener," it is the puzzlement of the realistic narrators that, combined with the increasingly symbolic nature of Roderick's "house" and Bartleby's "walls," that effect the transformation. The narrators in "Usher" and "Bartleby" make the ambiguity of the kind of fictional world both they and the readers inhabit an explicit part of the very plot of their stories.

Chapter 3

Nineteenth-Century Realism

The literary term realism was first used in the 1850s to describe Flaubert's focus on provincial life in his novel *Madame Bovary* and Turgenev's focus on peasant life in his short stories *A Sportsman's Sketches*. The movement came to America a decade later, where it was at first identified with local color or regionalism; much of the interest in American geographical locales depended on such realistic conventions as detailed physical description and the creation of culture-bound characters specific to such regions as New England, the South, and the emerging West. At the same time, though, a lingering romanticism often resulted in the sentimentalizing of the geographical areas and stereotyping of the characters native to them.

Bret Harte and Ambrose Bierce

The most important American regionalist short story writer during the period was Bret Harte, who combined elements of realism and romanticism in a way that was both popular and influential. Fred Lewis Pattee places Harte second only to Washington Irving in his influence on the development of the short story, claiming that Harte, while making use of paradox and antithesis and emphasizing technique over content, created individualized character types and gave the short story an atmosphere of locality as well as the saving grace of western humor.

Harte would have been happy to accept humor as his major contribution, for he singled it out as the factor that finally diminished the influence of the English novel on American fiction. It was a humor, Harte claimed, "of a quality as distinct and original as the country and civilization in which it was developed. . . . It was common in the barrooms, the gatherings in the 'country store,' and finally at public meetings in the mouths of 'stump orators.'"[1] The best example of how Harte's humorous viewpoint undercuts his surface sentimentality is one of his best-known stories, "Tennessee's Partner." After relating how Tennessee's partner went to San Francisco for a wife and was stopped in Stockton by a young waitress who broke at least two plates of toast over his head, the story's narrator says that he is well aware that "something more might be made of this episode, but I prefer to tell it as it was current at Sandy Bar—in the gulches and barrooms—where all sentiment was modified by a strong sense of humor." And it is from this point of view—sentiment tempered with humor—that Harte tells the central episode: Tennessee's running off with his partner's wife is related in the same flippant phrases used to describe his partner's somewhat hazardous wooing. Once we are willing to accept that this barroom point of view dominates the story, Harte's story becomes an occasion not for tears but for sardonic laughter.

The most accomplished practitioner of the sardonic story in the late nineteenth century was Ambrose Bierce, who pushed Poe's story of "effect" to self-conscious extremes. His most famous story, "An Occurrence at Owl Creek Bridge," is a pretext for a literary experiment with the convention of short story endings that Poe emphasized so strongly in his essay "The Poetic Principle." In Bierce's story, death is forestalled in the only way it can be—through an elaborate bit of fiction-making, which the reader initially takes to be actuality. "An Occurrence at Owl Creek Bridge" thematically and technically interrelates the idea of the reader's being pulled up short as the protagonist comes to the end of his rope and faces the ultimate and only "natural end"—death. At the end of Part I of the story, the narrator provides the reader with a clue to the story's manipulation of narrative time: "As these thoughts, which have here to be set down in words, were flashed into the doomed man's brain rather than evolved from it the captain nodded to the sergeant. The sergeant stepped aside." In this explicit, self-reflexive reference to the most notorious characteristic of fiction—the impossibility of escaping time—Bierce emphasizes the author's desire to communicate that which is timeless, even as he knows he is trapped by the time-bound nature of words that can only be told, or read, one after another.

The Trick-Ending Story

The exploitation of one of the short story's most characteristic conventions—its particular emphasis on closure—can also be seen in one of the most popular stories of the nineteenth century, Frank Stockton's "The Lady, or the Tiger."[2] The fact that this famous story seems to end before its actual conclusion, giving the reader the freedom to choose an ending, capitalizes on the reader's need to "close" a story—to see, in this instance, true justice satisfactorily enacted. Stockton urges readers to end the story not by choosing whether they want the lady or the tiger to come out of the doors, but rather by means of the way readers always achieve closure—by looking back at the plot, tone, and story motifs to determine the story's thematic purpose or "end." Since "The Lady, or the Tiger" makes quite clear that the semibarbaric nature of the princess consists of her being both ladylike and tigerlike, what readers are really asked to decide is which of these aspects of the princess dominates at the end. Because both the tone of the story and Stockton's choice of detail leaves little doubt as to which side that is, the reader is not so free to choose as it first appears.

The most influential manipulator of the short story's emphasis on closure is O. Henry, who experimented so frequently with ironic patterns that his name has become synonymous with the formulaic, trick-ending short story. His typical ironic structuring can be seen quite clearly in his well-known "The Cop and the Anthem," in which an elegant bum named Soapy tries to get himself thrown into jail but continually fails. The basic irony of the story is that so long as the erudite Soapy is "free," the threat of the coming winter negates his freedom; whereas if he were imprisoned, a state he actively seeks, he would indeed be "free" to enjoy life. However, Soapy does not want something for nothing: he is willing to "pay" for his room and board by going to some effort to commit an act that, according to the law, will earn him a warm place in jail. Of course, a story with an ironic, mocking tone such as this one can only end one way: Soapy, who does not want something for nothing, finally does get thrown into jail for doing precisely nothing.

O. Henry takes this kind of ironic short story as far as it can go, ultimately parodying the form he has mastered. Russian formalist critic B. M. Éjxenbaum cites O. Henry as a classic example of the formalist theory that "stages in the evolution of a genre can be observed when the genre, once utilized as an entirely serious or 'high' one, undergoes regeneration, coming out in parodic or comic form."[3] Éjxenbaum says that O. Henry's stories parody the ironically patterned short story form popular since Poe, thus, by exposing their conventions as artifice, paving the way for the more "realistic" stories of Anton Chekhov and James Joyce.

Henry James and Stephen Crane

Before Chekhov and Joyce revitalized the short story in the early decades of this century, it was the impressionism of Henry James and Stephen Crane that sustained the form during the late-nineteenth-century reign of the naturalistic novel. James argued that a work of narrative art is not a copy of life but rather "a personal, a direct impression of life," and he insisted on the self-conscious artistic control typical of the short story since Poe while focusing on the nature of everyday social reality, traditionally the subject of choice of the novel. "The Real Thing," one of James's best-known stories, is an important fictional treatment of just this tension between ordinary reality and artistic technique. The artist in the story insists so strongly on the social stereotype his models represent that he is unable to penetrate to the human reality beneath the surface. As James makes clear in his preface to the story, what he is interested in is the pattern or form of the work—its ability to transcend mere narrative and to communicate "something of the real essence of the subject."

Although James's artist claims that he cherishes "human accidents" and that what he hates most is being ridden by a type, the irony James explores in the story is that the only way an artist can communicate character is to create a patterned picture that illustrates something; in a story there can be no such thing as a "human accident." "The Real Thing" is constructed on a series of ambiguous antinomies in which our definition of what is real constantly changes: reality versus appearance, the real versus the representative, the real versus the unreal, the real versus the ideal, morality versus aesthetics, perfection versus imperfection, pride versus humility, interpretation versus imitation. If the artist's task is to perceive and reveal the real thing, which may lie beneath the surface of the apparent thing, then the painter in this story fails to be an artist, as he himself recognizes.

Many critics have argued that Stephen Crane's combination of the subjectivity of romanticism and the objectivity of realism marks the true beginnings of the modern short story in America. In one of Crane's best-known impressionistic stories, "The Blue Hotel," in which complex image patterns convey the formal and mechanical unreality of the events, the conflict between subjective and objective reality centers on the character of the Swede, whose reading of Western pulp fiction convinces him that he has entered into a fictional world that has become real. When the hotel owner Scully tries to convince him that the town is civilized and real rather than barbaric and fictional, and that what he thought was reality—the childlike world of the pulp Western—was a game after all, the Swede is transformed and decides to "play" the game; instead of being a stranger to the conventions he thought existed in the hotel, he becomes familiar and at home with them—too much at home.

A card game forms the center of the story and leads to its violent climax when the Swede, following the conventions of the Western novel, accuses Johnny of cheating, even though the game is "only for fun." The Swede wins the conventional fight that follows because of the superiority of his new viewpoint; he can now self-consciously play the fictional game that Johnny and the others take seriously—while they rage with impotent anger, he only laughs. The final irony takes place when the Swede, still within the conventions of the game, leaves the hotel and enters a bar. When he tries to bully the gambler into drinking with him, the gambler, being a professional who does not "play for fun," stabs the Swede, who falls with a "cry of supreme astonishment." Thus, the Swede's premonition at the beginning of the story is fulfilled, though in a different way from what he imagined: his initial "error" about the place is not an error at all—rather, it is in fact a violent and barbaric world.

A central problem for nineteenth-century short story writers was how to communicate realistically the secret psychic life formerly presented allegorically in the mythic romance. In the older tale or romance, characters functioned as psychic projections of basic human fears and desires; in the new fiction, however, the characters had to be presented as if they were real. As we have seen, in "Young Goodman Brown" Hawthorne combined both allegorical and realistic elements in an ambiguous mix of dream and reality. In "The Fall of the House of Usher," Poe presented a real character entering the artwork's hermetically sealed world dominated by an obsessed and ultimately metaphoric character. And in "Bartleby the Scrivener," Melville moved closer to realistic conventions by beginning with what appears to be the "real world" and then presenting that world as having been invaded by a metaphoric character who transforms reality into metaphor. The problem for all three of these early narrative experimentalists was how to bridge the gap between romance conventions in which characters *embody* psychic states and realistic conventions in which they *possess* psychic states.

Joseph Conrad

Joseph Conrad confronts this problem explicitly in his two most famous short works. In "Heart of Darkness" he creates a world like that of "Young Goodman Brown," in which the landscape symbolically represents the ultimate reaches of psychic reality. Moreover, he develops a plot structure very much like that in Poe's "The Fall of the House of Usher" and Melville's "Bartleby the Scrivener": a realistic narrator confronts a metaphoric extremist.

In "The Secret Sharer," Conrad seeks a way to enable a central character to deal with an inner conflict by projecting that conflict outside of himself. The captain in Conrad's story is Hamlet-like in his preoccupation with his own lack of definition. Thus, much as Hamlet creates a play within a play to project his conflict outward so that he can cope with it, Conrad's young captain creates the character of Leggatt to provide him with the means by which he can deal with his own insecurity and establish his own identity.

Conrad pushes to metaphoric extremes a common psychological phenomenon wherein an inner conflict creates a split in the self, so that it seems as if there are two separate voices engaged in a dialogue with each other. Leggatt, whose name suggests he is a "legate" or emissary, is the objectified side of the captain's Hamlet-like, preoccupied, subjective self. The story, then, is split between the plot, which focuses on the captain's efforts to protect and conceal the mysterious stranger, and the mind of the captain, who obsessively persists in perceiving and describing the stranger as his other self, his double.

Although Frederick Karl says the constant repetition of the similarity between the captain and Leggatt is tedious and the weakest part of the work, Conrad himself felt that every word in the story fit perfectly without "a single uncertain note."[4] The constant repetition that Karl and others have found so obvious is perhaps a purposeful tactic on Conrad's part to suggest both that Leggatt is a romance-like symbolic projection of the captain's psyche and, at the same time, a real character with his own objective existence to whom the captain reacts in an obsessive way.

The story begins with the central motif of the captain's lack of identity. He says he is not only a stranger on the ship but also a stranger to himself, and he wonders if he will "turn out faithful to that ideal conception of one's own personality every man sets up for himself secretly."[5] And indeed, many metaphorical details in the story suggest Leggatt has been summoned forth from the captain's unconscious as an aspect of the self with which he must deal. For example, Leggatt is first seen as a silvery, fishlike naked body emerging from the sea to whom the captain responds in a matter-of-fact way, as if he were expecting him. The image of the captain looking straight down into a face upturned exactly under his own is clearly an allusion to the myth of Narcissus. The variation Conrad works on the myth is that the captain does not fall into his reflection; rather, the reflection, as in a number of German romantic tales, comes out of the mirror-like sea and takes on a problematic, independent existence. After Leggatt puts on one of the captain's sleeping suits, the captain says, it was "as though I had been faced by my own reflection in the depths of a somber and immense mirror" ("Secret Sharer," 9).

The basic psychological and moral issues the story deals with are the following: What does it mean to be a stranger to yourself? What does it mean to see yourself in another? What does it mean to be your brother's keeper? What does "being in command" mean? What does the phenomenon of talking to oneself suggest? Why does having a secret self split the self? Because of the story's complexity, "The Secret Sharer" can be read in any one of several different ways. Although it follows the conventions of a sea adventure story, it can also be read as a story of initiation in which the captain must meet the challenge of command and move from insecurity to confidence in his own ability. Moreover, even as it can be discussed as a story of moral conflict in which the captain must make a decision between identifying with the individual or with the rules created by society, it can also be read as a story of psychological projection in which Leggatt represents certain aspects of the captain's own personality—aspects with which he must come to terms. Because Leggatt is both inside the captain and outside him, there is no real inconsistency in these various interpretations. As the captain says, "I was constantly watching myself, my secret self, as dependent on my actions as my own personality" ("Secret Sharer," 17).

Albert Guerard, in his discussion of the story as a dramatization of the archetypal myth of the night journey, suggests that Conrad here intended the sea from which Leggatt climbs as a symbol of the unconscious.[6] However, the difference between the way Conrad's story handles the night journey myth and the way old romance forms typically handle it is that, in Conrad's story, both the captain and Leggatt are presented as if they have an objective existence in the world. Yet, even though Leggatt seems to be objectively real, he is the self-conscious image of the fictional character as an authorial projection. Although we must assume that others have seen him as an objective presence in the world before the story begins, no one but the captain sees him during the actual events of the story. All we know of Leggatt outside of the young captain's moral/mirror relationship with him is through his and Captain Archbold's stories—which differ in important details. The anecdote of the scorpion in the inkwell is the *mise en abyme*, the point of reflexive self-reference, of "The Secret Sharer," for it is here that we see the entire story reflected in miniature. Leggatt comes out of the inky water of the sea, which represents both the unconscious of the captain/Conrad and the inkwell source of all stories; the Ocean of Story is both the ocean of the unconscious and the inkwell. At the end of "The Secret Sharer," Leggatt's movement back into the sea, representing the captain's reintegration of the split in his self, is his movement back into the inkwell. Leggatt, the oneiric creation of both the captain and the artist, says, "I am off the face of the earth now. As I came at night so shall I go" ("Secret Sharer," 29). The captain says his situation vis-à-vis Leggatt is like being mad, only worse, because he is aware of it: it is as though the captain has developed a schizophrenic split but is nevertheless able to observe it and to cope with it because it has been displaced outside of the self. The effect in "The Secret Sharer" is much like what is now called lucid dreaming, in which the dreamer, aware that he or she is dreaming, is to some extent able to manipulate the dream's events. And just as dreams work out conflicts that one cannot work out in conscious life, so also does Conrad's dreamlike fiction work out or objectify the inner conflict of the captain, whose narrative task is to develop a sense of self.

Making manifest that which is hidden is the primary structural force of "The Secret Sharer." This objectification of inner reality marks the beginning of the modern mythical method of fictional narration, as Thomas Mann defines it in his famous essay "Freud and the Future." Mann explicitly calls for a modern fiction that mixes the psychological and the mythical, for he affirms as truth the observation—important both to Arthur Schopenhauer and to Sigmund Freud—that life itself is a "mingling of the individual elements and the formal stock-in-trade; a mingling in which the individual, as it were, only lifts his head above the formal and impersonal elements." Much of the "extra-personal," Mann insists, "much unconscious identification, much that is conventional and schematic, is none the less decisive for the experience not only of the artist but of the human being in general."[7]

Mann implies that our interest in fictional characters, regardless of the events in which they are enmeshed, is always located in the process by which they try to find their identity, the means by which they attempt to answer the age-old Oedipal question, "Who am I?" In such a process the two forces of the subjective and the schematic are decisive. As Robert Langbaum has described it, when one realizes that introspection leads to nothing but endless reflection, one sees that the only way to discover one's identity is to don a mask and step into a story. "The point," says Langbaum, "is at that level of experience where events fall into a pattern . . . they are an objectification of your deepest will, since they make you do things other than you consciously intend; so that in responding like a marionette to the necessities of the story, you actually find out what you really want and who you really are."[8] This creation of an "as-if-real" character to embody psychic processes marks the impressionistic extension of the romantic trend that began the short story form earlier in the nineteenth century.

Anton Chekhov

The most influential "impressionist" short story writer to gain critics' attention is Anton Chekhov. An anonymous reviewer in 1903 remarked that it was Chekhov's "impressionism" and "his perfection of form" that most characterized his work.[9] Whereas some critics found that Chekhov's lack of incident and avoidance of denouement made his tales lack every element that constitute a really good short story, others saw this as his chief merit and delighted in his genius at presenting a "fugitive impression focussed with the swiftness of a snapshot" (*Critical Heritage*, 72).

Although some of Chekhov's stories appeared in translation in America in 1891 and in England in 1897, it was not until the anthologies translated by Marian Fell and Adeline Lister Kays appeared in 1914 and 1915 that he began to be recognized by such reviewers as E. M. Forster in England and H. S. Canby in America as a striking challenge to the snappy-ending stories common in both countries' magazines at the time. The thirteen volumes translated by Constance Garnett between 1916 and 1922 reaffirmed this realization and firmly established Chekhov as one of the great short story writers of his time, as well as the creator of a distinctive new short story form.

In 1899, American novelist Abraham Cahan said that one of the most striking features of Chekhov's stories was their "naturalness," that his genius was best seen in stories that are so "absolutely storyless that there is not enough even to fill a nutshell." In 1915 literary historian H. S. Canby argued that while American stories, à la O. Henry, were based on literary convention, Chekhov's stories were based on life. Joining the chorus of writers and critics who welcomed Chekhov's realism because it rescued the short story from the pattern of artificial irony that had overcome it, Leonard Woolf suggested that Chekhov had the ability to show "exactly what a little piece of life is like," and E. M. Forster noted that Chekhov's highest gift was negative, in that he did not write stories with the conventional snap (*Critical Heritage*, 134, 162, 138). Gradually, some critics began to suspect that more art was involved in Chekhov's stories than appeared on their deceptively casual surface. In addition to calling him a realist, for example, E. M. Forster suggested that Chekhov was primarily a poet. John Middleton Murry argued that Chekhov's stories were more "nakedly aesthetic" than those of any writer before him (*Critical Heritage*, 205); Conrad Aiken claimed that Chekhov's genius was primarily lyrical in that he manipulated feeling or mood rather than plot or thought.[10]

The Chekhovian shift to the "modern" short story is marked by a continuation of the shift from the romantic focus on projective fiction, in which characters are functions in an essentially code-bound parabolic structure, to an apparently realistic episode in which plot is subordinate to "as-if-real" character. However, Chekhov's fictional figures are not realistic in the way that characters in the novel usually are. The short story is too compressed to allow the creation of characters through multiplicity of detail and social interaction, as is typical of the novel. Once we see that the short story, by its very brevity, cannot deal with the dense detail and duration in the way that a novel can, but instead must focus on a revelatory breakup of the rhythm of everyday reality, we see how the form, striving to accommodate "realism" at the end of the nineteenth century, focused on an

experience under the influence of a particular mood and therefore depended more on tone than on plot as a principle of
unity.

In one of Chekhov's best-known stories, "Misery" (sometimes
translated as "Lament" or "Heartache"), the everyday rhythm of
the old cab driver's reality is suggested by his two different fares,
a rhythm he tries to break into by telling his fares that his son is
dead. The story would indeed be only a sketch if the cab driver
did not tell his story to the little mare at the end—for what the
story presents is the comic and pathetic sense of the incommunicable nature of grief itself. Caught by the basic desire to tell a
story of the breakup of his everyday reality that will express the
irony he senses, and that, by being deliberate and detailed, will
both express his grief and control it, he "thirsts for speech" and
wants to tell his story "properly, with deliberation."

Although "Misery" is a lament, it is not an emotional wailing
but, rather, a controlled objectification of grief by the deliberate
presentation of details. It therefore indicates in a basic way one
of the primary contributions Chekhov makes to the short story:
the expression of a complex inner state by presenting selected
concrete details rather than by developing either a parabolic
form or by depicting the mind of the character. Significant reality
for Chekhov is inner rather than outer reality; but the problem
then becomes one of creating the illusion of inner reality by
focusing on externals only. The answer for the modern short
story is to find a story that, if expressed "properly"—that is, by
the judicious choice of relevant details—will embody the complexity of the inner state. T. S. Eliot would later term such a technique "objective correlative," and James Joyce would master it
fully in *Dubliners*.

Although Sean O'Faolain has called Chekhov's "Gooseberries" one of the most perfect stories in the whole of the
world's literature," describing that perfection is not so easy.
Certainly, it does not depend on the creation of plot or character,
for nothing "happens" in the story, and the characters are little
else than tellers of or listeners to the story. What makes "Gooseberries" a typical "modern" short story is its self-conscious focus
on how such a modern story communicates.

First of all, "Gooseberries" makes use of the device of a story
within a story, an "ancient, ubiquitous, and persistent" conven-

tion that John Barth has called "almost as old and various . . . as the narrative impulse itself."[11] Barth agrees with his mentor Jorge Luis Borges that such framed tales often focus on the nature of storytelling and on the fictional nature of reality itself. Chekhov's primary interest in "Gooseberries" lies in the relationship between the inner and the outer tale, a fact he announces early by having Ivan begin to tell his story on the road, only to have it immediately interrupted by a sudden rain. This tactic shifts the framework or context for the story out of the external "real" world into the unreal upstairs showroom of Aloyhin. There both teller and audience, having bathed and put on warm, dry clothes to be served by the beautiful servant Pelageya, can escape into a stereotype of the nineteenth-century bourgeois world of the sitting room, where stories that have nothing to do with one's own immediate reality can be told, heard, and read. As Ivan tells his story, it is as though the ladies and military men in the portraits on the wall are also part of the audience.

The story Ivan tells is in many ways a conventional illustrative story with a moral tag at the end. Yet neither *what* the story illustrates nor *how* it does so is so conventional. Although Ivan's story is about his brother achieving his dream to own land, he says that it is not his brother but himself that he wishes to talk about. And what he wishes to discuss is the paradox that happiness makes him sad. Like the narrator in Melville's "Bartleby the Scrivener," who says that because "misery hides aloof, we deem that misery there is none," Ivan says, "we do not see or hear those who suffer, and what is terrible in life goes on somewhere behind the scenes." Also as in "Bartleby," although Ivan believes in charity and love in the abstract, he declares he can do nothing about it but grieve inwardly. Lamenting, "Oh, if I were young," he tells his host, "There is no happiness and there should be none, and if life has a meaning and a purpose, that meaning and purpose is not our happiness but something greater and more rational. Do good!"

Just as it is not the so-called humane passage in Gogol's famous "The Overcoat" that makes his story a masterpiece but, rather, the story's interplay of folktale conventions and an ironic teller, so also the perfection of "Gooseberries" does not derive from the moral injunction to "do good" or to seek the meaning of life in something "greater and more rational" than happiness.

Rather, what constitutes the story's subtlety is the inescapable irony of Ivan's situation, in which even as he denies happiness, he delights in it—delights in the refreshing bath and the swim, delights in the warm clothes and the beautiful Pelageya, delights in crawling into the wide, cool beds that smell of clean linen.

As Mark Schorer points out, at the end of "Gooseberries," when Aloyhin goes back downstairs to the world of reality, glad that the story has had nothing to do with his own life, Burkin cannot sleep because of the unidentifiable smell of Ivan's pipe that he lighted when he first began his story. "It is the smell of some lingering falsehood, of Ivan's story," says Schorer,

> which tried at once to prove and disprove its point. The frame of the story—the landscape, the arrival, the farm, the bath, and the swim, the downstairs and the upstairs rooms, the sleep at last—all these have proved the proving-disproving attempt. The frame has judged the anecdote; its actuality reveals the confusion of fact and dream in the anecdote it contains.[12]

Ivan's story may be an anecdote with a didactic purpose, but Chekhov's story depends neither on anecdote nor on event; nor, as he frequently insisted, does it mean to teach. Rather, "Gooseberries" is characterized by Chekhov's objectivity and his delicate use of the convention of the frame tale, wherein the inner story is undercut by the outer one. Chekhov once said that it might be pleasant to "combine a story with a sermon, but for me personally it is extremely difficult and most impossible owing to conditions of technique."[13] And that technique, as Conrad Aiken was the first to note, is not to manipulate thought as James did or plot as Poe did, but rather to manipulate feeling or mood. As Prince D. S. Mirsky says, Chekhov's stories are not so much narrative as they are musical; they are bathed in a "perfect and uniform haze" (*Critical Heritage*, 323). Such a concept of story as an impressionistic, hazy, eventless evocation of mood has been characteristic of the modern notion of story since Conrad; the meaning of a story for Conrad's storyteller persona Marlowe "was not inside like a kernel but outside, enveloping the tale which brought it out only as a glow brings out a haze."

Like Chekhov, whom she greatly admired, Katherine Mansfield was often accused of writing sketches instead of stories because her works did not manifest the plotted action of nineteenth-century short fiction. The best-known Mansfield story similar in technique and theme to the typical Chekhov story is "The Fly," the external action of which is extremely slight. The unnamed "boss" is visited by a retired friend whose casual mention of the boss's dead son makes him aware of his inability to grieve. The story ends with the boss idly dropping ink on a fly until it dies, whereupon he flings it away. Like Chekhov's "Misery," this story about the nature of grief maintains a strictly objective point of view, allowing concrete details to communicate the significance of the boss's emotional state.

However, Mansfield differs from Chekhov by emphasizing the fly itself as an ambiguous symbol of the death of the boss's grief, his own manipulated son, or the trivia of life that distracts him from feeling. Moreover, instead of focusing on the inarticulate nature of grief that goes deeper than words, "The Fly" seems to emphasize the transitory nature of grief: regardless of how much the boss would like to hold on to his grief for his son, he finds it increasingly difficult to maintain such feelings. Such an inevitable loss of grief does not necessarily suggest that the boss's feelings for his son are negligible; rather, it suggests a subtle aspect of grief—that it either flows naturally or else it must be self-consciously and artificially sought after. The subtle way in which Mansfield communicates the complexity of the boss's emotional situation by the seemingly irrelevant conversation between the boss and his old acquaintance, as well as by his apparently idle toying with the fly, is typical of the Chekhovian device of allowing objective detail to communicate complex states of feeling.

James Joyce

The most influential modern writer to work in the Chekhovian mode is James Joyce. Although Joyce himself said that he never read Chekhov before he wrote *Dubliners*, such writers and critics as Richard Ellmann, Caroline Gordon, and Allen Tate have noted that Joyce's stories, particularly "The Dead," are Chekhovian in technique. This is not to suggest that Joyce lied about not reading Chekhov, but that during the first two decades of the twentieth century both Chekhov and Joyce were part of the modernist shift toward fiction in which realistic detail acquired metaphoric meaning through aesthetic patterning. Joyce's most famous contribution to the theory and technique of modern narrative is his notion of the "epiphany," which he explicitly defined in his early novel *Steven Hero*: "By an epiphany he meant a sudden spiritual manifestation, whether in the vulgarity of speech or of gesture or in a memorable phrase of the mind itself. He believed that it was for the man of letters to record these epiphanies with extreme care, seeing that they themselves are the most delicate and evanescent of moments."[14] In a Joyce story, and in many stories by other writers since Joyce, an epiphany is a formulation through metaphor or symbol of some revelatory aspect of human experience, some extremely significant aspect of personal reality; it is usually communicated by a pattern of what otherwise would be seen as trivial details and events.

Although any story in *Dubliners* might serve to illustrate Joyce's epiphany technique, his most famous story, "The Dead," is perhaps the clearest and most subtle example. The primary structural movement of the story—from the objective world of the Christmas party to the lyrical quality initiated by Gabriel's physical or aesthetic desire for his wife—carries through to the story's poetic end. This movement is paralleled by a transition in Gabriel himself, from self-assertion to self-effacement. The first two-thirds of the story reads as if it were a section from a novel written in the leisurely Dickensian mode: numerous characters are introduced, and the details of the party are given in great detail. It is only in the story's final third, when Gabriel's life is transformed—first by his romantic and sexual fantasy about his wife, then by his confrontation with her secret life—that the reader reflects back on the first part and perceives that the earlier concrete details and trivial remarks are symbolically significant. "The Dead" is a striking example of how, in short fiction, it is the end that lends significance to all that preceded it.

Joyce confronted two basic narrative problems in "The Dead": How is it possible for a realistic narrative to convey theme? And how can a story without a plot come to an end? The first problem is the same that Chekhov faced—how one can arrange concrete metonymic details in such a way that they develop into a pattern that is equivalent to theme. The second is a function of Joyce's notion of epiphany, which suggests that the story achieves closure either in retrospect, by the realization of a character or by the reader's absorbing of the story in such a way that the mere temporal events are transformed into a meaningful pattern.

Most critics agree with David Daiches's opinion that "The Dead" is the "working-out, in terms of realistic narrative, of a preconceived theme" of a man's "withdrawal into the circle of his own egotism" until the walls around him are broken down by the "culminating assault on his egotism, coming simultaneously from without, as an incident affecting him, and from within, as an increase in understanding."[15] However, Joyce's achievement in this story and its contribution to the development of the short story as a genre may be better understood if we see the story's most basic theme as the difference between the kind of reality that realistic prose imitates and the kind of reality that romantic prose reveals.

Anyone reading this story for the first time might be hard pressed to understand its fame and influence. The opening descriptions seem lengthy enough that the story could go on and on, ending only naturalistically with the end of the party. However, it is with the end of the party, of course, that the lyrical nature of the story begins to emerge. Thematically, the conflict in "The Dead" that reflects its realistic/lyrical split is the difference revealed to both Gabriel and the reader between public life and private life, between life as it is in actual experience and life perceived as desire.

The section of "The Dead" devoted to the party is the story of Gabriel's public life. As far as he is concerned, no one else has a private life, and his chief psychic interest lies in what kind of figure he will cut in public. However, throughout this section, there are moments—particularly those focusing on the past, on music, and on marital union—when reality is presented not as here and now but as a mixture of memory and desire. Thematically, the basic issue the story poses is: In which one of these realms does true reality reside?

Gabriel discovers at the end of the story not only that his wife has an inner life that is inaccessible to him but also that his own life has been an outer life only. This is all the more devastating to him because, on the journey to the hotel, he has indulged in his own self-delusion about their relationship: "moments of their secret life together burst like stars upon his memory. . . . Like the tender fires of stars moments of their life together that no one knew of or would ever know of, broke upon and illuminated his memory. He longed to recall to her those moments, to make her forget the years of their dull existence together and remember only their moments of ecstasy."[16]

Filled with desire and the memory of intimacy, and wishing Gretta to be at one with him, Gabriel is annoyed that she seems so distracted. When he discovers that she has a secret life that has nothing to do with him, he tries to use his typical public devices of irony—but the very simplicity of her story undercuts the effort, and he comes to see the inadequacy of his public self. Michael Furey, Gretta's young admirer, who has been willing to give his life for love of another, challenges Gabriel's own smug safety in much the same way that Bartleby challenges the narrator in Melville's famous story.

In the much-discussed lyrical ending of "The Dead," Gabriel confronts the irony that the dead Michael is more alive than he himself is. "Generous tears" fill his eyes because he knows that he has never lived the life of desire, but only the untransformed life of the everyday. The ending, in which Gabriel, awake and alone while his wife sleeps beside him, loses himself and imaginatively merges into a mythic lyrical sense of oneness, makes it possible for the reader to begin the story over again with the end in mind. "The Dead" cannot be understood in the way that most novels are read, one thing after another; rather, it exemplifies the way in which the modern short story must be read—as aesthetically patterned in such a way that only the end makes the rest of the story meaningful.

Sherwood Anderson

The double theme of the inaccessibility of the private life and the inadequacy of the public life is a common one in modern short fiction. It is most emphatically explored in the American equivalent of *Dubliners*, Sherwood Anderson's *Winesburg, Ohio*.[17] In the 100-year period between Washington Irving's *The Sketchbook* and Anderson's *Winesburg, Ohio*, the short story form changed from primarily a folktale genre to a form that focused more on lyric moments of realization than linear events. In his study of Anderson, Rex Burbank notes the influence of impressionism and post-impressionism on the stories in *Winesburg, Ohio*. He points out that the narratives stem from the flow of feeling and impressions rather than from any chronological ordering; their structure is psychological rather than chronological. What holds them together is a series of disconnected images that unite because they are thematically and symbolically related. In his *Memoirs*, Anderson writes, "There are no plot stories in life."

Burbank asserts that "Hands" is one of the best tales in *Winesburg, Ohio* and one of the most influenced by the postimpressionists. He notes the central image of the hands and how incidents charge the image with meaning.[18] Sister M. Joselyn discusses "Hands" as a central example of Anderson's development of what she terms the lyrical story: "Normal time sequence is almost obliterated as Anderson penetrates with the reader further and further into the mysterious recesses of Wing Biddlebaum's mind." She points out that the events of Biddlebaum's life are presented neither straightforwardly nor by means of a conventional flashback but rather by means of a box-within-a-box structure: Biddlebaum is revealed first through the eyes of the townspeople, then through the eyes of George Willard, and finally through his own sense of self. All these perspectives, she argues, are so thoroughly suffused with Biddlebaum's consciousness that we are not aware of any awkward juncture between sections.[19]

David Anderson says that what Anderson achieves in "Hands" is the transformation of a "poor little man, beaten, pounded, frightened by the world in which he lived, into something oddly beautiful."[20] The most frequent remark made about the characters in *Winesburg, Ohio* is that they are psychic deformities, cut off from society, adrift in their own consciousness, unfulfilled metaphors for American estrangement. In his book *The Lonely Voice*, Frank O'Connor uses Anderson's collection as a central example of his notion of short story characters representing not individuals but submerged population groups.

Anderson's suggestion in the story—that the secret of Biddlebaum's hands is a job for a poet to describe—is part of the basic change in the short story signaled by Chekhov. Anderson struggles with the problem of the prose writer trying to communicate something subtle and delicate, feeling the words are clumsy, for all he has are the events and explanation. What he needs is to use language the way the poet does, a way to transcend language. This is why the central metaphor of this story is "talking with hands": the use of hands as a central image also suggests many other implications, such as the magic of "laying on of hands," "keep your hands off," maintaining "clean hands," and so on. Biddlebaum wants to transcend the physical, but the only way he can touch someone is with hands, which by their very nature are physical; thus, their touch is inevitably ambiguous.

The problem the narrator of the story faces is in trying to express the kind of love Wing has for the boys without its sounding crude or being misunderstood; it is not flesh but spirit that is at stake here, and spirit is difficult to communicate. Motifs throughout the story—notably, dreams becoming facts for the half-witted boy and doubts becoming beliefs for the men of the town—suggest this counterpoint between the spiritual and the physical. At the end of "Hands," when Biddlebaum performs the mundane task of picking up crumbs, the gesture is transformed into a spiritual act.

The technique Anderson uses here is similar to that used by Chekhov and Joyce. For modern short story writers, intangible spiritual desires and feelings are contaminated by the material, but both the characters in these stories and their authors must accept the fact that they have only the material with which to communicate desires and feelings. The task of finding concrete ways to communicate emotional states becomes the central problem for most short story writers in the twentieth century.

Chapter 4

EARLY-TWENTIETH-CENTURY FORMALISM

Sherwood Anderson's *Winesburg, Ohio* (1919) appeared exactly one hundred years after the publication of Washington Irving's *The Sketchbook*. In the intervening period the short story changed fundamentally, from a folktale or romance genre to a realistic form that communicates meaning primarily by carefully patterned detail rather than by anecdotal events told in a linear fashion. Yet the short story never fully forgot its mythic-romantic background. During the forty years following *Winesburg, Ohio* the form evolved by means of a competitive interrelationship between the formal methods of Chekhovian realism and the romance themes of Hawthorne and Poe transplanted into the twentieth-century milieu. This basic duality can be seen in the difference between Hemingway's radical extension of Chekhov's ironic understatement and William Faulkner's creation of a self-contained mythic world; between Katherine Anne Porter's tightly structured Joycean explorations of the meaning of memory and Eudora Welty's creation of a fairy tale–like "season of dreams"; between John Cheever's controlled evocation of the world of the suburban middle class and Flannery O'Connor's moral romances of the rural South.

Ernest Hemingway

Although Hemingway said his greatest debt was to Turgenev, his famous "objective" style is more obviously an extension of Chekhov. There is a clear relationship between Chekhov's sense that "in short stories it is better to say not enough than to say too much" and Hemingway's conviction that a writer "may omit things that he knows and the reader, if the writer is writing truly enough, will have a feeling of those things as strongly as though the writer had stated them."[1] This assumption is quite evident in Hemingway's "Big Two-Hearted River," in which seemingly realistic descriptive details metaphorically objectify Nick's psychic distress rather than mimetically create a sense of the external world. Thus, at the end of Hemingway's story, Nick's refusal to go into the swamp is a purely metaphoric refusal, having nothing to do with the real qualities of the swamp, only its metaphoric qualities—that is, the swamp's embodiment of his own psychic state.

"Hills Like White Elephants" is perhaps an even clearer example of Hemingway's Chekhovian style, for it is his most complex "minimal" story, and in many ways seems a self-conscious experiment in pushing Chekhov's techniques as far as they can go. On the one hand, there seems little in the story that is not conflict, since the disagreement between the man and woman constitutes its only action. At the same time, though, the nature of that conflict is left so vague that it can only be designated by the impersonal pronoun "it." The man insists, "It's not really anything," "It's perfectly natural," and "It's perfectly simple." The woman says, "If I do it you'll be happy and things will be like they were," "If I do it you won't ever worry," and "Then I'll do it. Because I don't care about it."[2]

Although it gradually becomes clear that the "it" passages cited above refer to the abortion the man wants the woman to have, other references to "it" in the story refer to the pregnancy. The man says at one point, "It's the only thing that's made us unhappy," and later, "I'm perfectly willing to go through with it if it means anything to you." The woman, in turn, responds, "Doesn't it mean anything to you? We could get along." Finally, still a third reference to "it" occurs when the woman walks to the end of the station and looks across the river and says, "And we could have everything and every day we make it more impossible." To the man's assurance, "We can have the whole world," she responds, "It isn't ours any more. . . . Once they take it away, you never get it back."

Communicating the emotional complexity of the conflict between the man and woman without giving the terms of that conflict a name other than the indefinite pronoun "it" is the formal challenge Hemingway tackles in the story, first, by transforming the very spatial-temporal status of the story into a metaphor of the couple's conflict; and second, by presenting that conflict in terms of what he sees as a gender-based tension between looking at the world metaphorically and looking at it pragmatically and realistically. From Hemingway's viewpoint, the pregnant woman wants the child for emotional reasons, whereas the man wants her to have the abortion for purely practical ones.

The temporal structure of the story is announced twice—at the beginning, when we learn that the train from Barcelona will arrive in forty minutes, and at the end, when we learn that the train will arrive in five minutes. In this "between trains" situation cut off from the ordinary flow of time, Hemingway explicitly announces that the events of the story take place in a time span of thirty-five minutes. However, once we learn that the dialogue, which constitutes the entire story, takes only fifteen minutes to deliver realistically, we have the legitimate right to ask what happened to the missing twenty minutes. If Hemingway had not wanted us to be aware of this discrepancy, he would not have established the time frame so explicitly in the first place, or he would have made the time span of the events more closely match the time span of the reading. The missing twenty minutes constitute that part of the iceberg in Hemingway's famous metaphor that is underwater; they occupy the blank spaces between the lines of the story, those moments when the characters have nothing to say.

Hemingway makes the spatial status of the story as explicit as the temporal status. The first paragraph locates the couple at a junction situated between two lines of rails, one line going the way they have come, the other going in the direction in which they are heading. And where they are going, metaphorically, is precisely what is at issue in the story: the man wants to go one way, and the woman wants to go another. Hemingway also states explicitly that they are in a valley with barren hills on one side and the green fields on the other side, a spatial location that reflects their conflict. The reader is first made aware of their conflict when the woman says the hills look like white elephants, to which the man replies that he has never seen one; but the conflict gradually reveals itself to be a profound difference in worldview. On the one hand, hers is an idle remark, probably the kind of remark she has perhaps made many times in the past in their travels as they look around at the landscape and comment on it. Yet what makes this more than an idle remark here is the fact that the man does not respond to it in the way he probably did in the past. Instead of looking at something with her, he is focused on himself and his concern with "it."

The metaphoric location of the couple, between their past and their future, is related to the fact that there are so many silences in their conversation, as well as to their disagreement about the white elephants—which starts the conflict moving. When two people feel at "at one" with each other, they can make trivial comments with the full confidence that the remarks will be appreciated by the other. If that sense of union is broken, though, silly remarks fall flat. It is as if there is nothing to say—something the woman is painfully aware of when, absolutely out of patience with the man's "reasonableness," she says, "Would you please please please please please please please stop talking?"

The conflict between them is also manifested in the very language of the story. Whereas the woman often uses metaphoric language, the man uses the language of logic and reason. When she says that everything tastes like licorice, she seems to have some meaning in mind, for she generalizes by saying, "especially all the things you've waited so long for, like absinthe." Whether the woman is making a conscious reference to the bitter sweetness of their situation, we know that the pregnancy has this same bittersweet effect, for even as it suggests their union, it also suggests their point of contention and thus their separation. The central metaphor of the white elephants, of course, reflects their basic situation—for a white elephant is, in some Eastern cultures, an animal that is both precious and useless at the same time. The unnamed "it" in the story is, like the taste of licorice and a white elephant, valuable and sweet but also worthless and bitter.

The basic situation in the story, although it seems puzzling at first, can now be seen in all its complexity. The woman wants to have the baby; the man does not. However, more than this, the woman wants the man to want to have the baby; he, on the other hand, wants her to want to have the operation. He says he does not want her to go through with it if she does not want to, but the point is, of course, that he wants her to want to. In such a situation as this, talk is pointless; arguing is certainly pointless. He uses logic, providing several reasons she should have an abortion; she, however, can only speak from emotion, using not logic but metaphor, metaphor with which he can no longer identify or sympathize.

At the end of the story, when the train's arrival is announced, the man picks up the bags and carries them across the station to the other tracks; as he stops to buy another drink, a drink that tastes like licorice, he looks at the people waiting "reasonably" for the train, for he does not understand why she is not "reasonable." However, there is no way to argue reasonably about the conflict at the center of the story. Whatever sense of union the couple once had is gone; and once it is gone, as the woman knows, one cannot get it back. Although we know that the two people will be going in the same direction physically at the end of the story, we know that they will be going in opposite directions emotionally.

As this brief analysis of one of Hemingway's paradigmatic short stories has tried to indicate, Hemingway's style is an extension of Chekhov's and Joyce's attempts to make what at first seems to be merely a realistic depiction of ordinary physical reality communicate metaphorically the extraordinary human complexity of what is, basically, incommunicable. Just as the gooseberries in Chekhov's story of that name become a metaphor of the bitter sweetness of Ivan's inexpressible realization, and the snow in Joyce's "The Dead" comes to represent death and the loss of self, so also do the simple details in Hemingway's seemingly realistic story become transformed into embodiments of complex human conflict.

Katherine Anne Porter

This same metaphorical technique can be seen in the stories of Katherine Anne Porter. Because her primary muse is that of history or memory, her stories, even as they maintain Hemingway's Chekhovian formal style, are more aligned with the symbolic notion of myth or story. One of her most Hemingway-like stories is "Theft." As is usual in post-Chekhovian stories, there is no explicit background exposition in this story to suggest the conflict of the female protagonist, except for the oblique reference to a letter she has received that has made her decide to end the relationship. The contents of the letter constitute an appropriate metaphor for modern short fiction, for it is largely made up of blanks, gaps, ellipses. However, by "reading between the lines," we suspect the letter signals a broken relationship—a suspicion that is further suggested by her telling the janitress that the purse the older woman stole was a present from someone and that losing it makes her feel as though she has been robbed of an enormous number of valuable things.

Most of the story focuses on the seemingly irrelevant encounters she recalls from the "immediate past": the polite ceremonies of Camilo as he tries to put on a good front, and then hiding his hat under his coat to save it from the rain; her conversation with Roger in the taxi about trying to make up his mind to do something definite regarding his relationship with a young woman; the dialogue with Bill, who complains that his wife is ruining him with her extravagance, and who cannot pay the protagonist what he owes her. In the midst of these scenes, others "in passing," as it were, focus momentarily on three boys who talk about getting married, and on two girls, one of whom complains about the conflicts of her relationship. What unites all these seemingly unrelated scenes is that all focus on broken, flawed, or faulty relationships in which people are posturing or putting on a false front.

Given this background, it seems inevitable that when the protagonist confronts the janitress to get her purse back, she will realize the justness of the janitress' rebuke, that she has already let her chances pass her by. Thus, the story very economically and indirectly conveys a life lived carelessly; as the janitress says, "you leave things around and don't seem to notice much." As the protagonist realizes, life is a process of having things taken from you, but the worst kind of loss results from one's own neglect and failure to take care of oneself—for it is this kind of loss that ends by leaving one with nothing.

Eudora Welty has said that Porter, by using only enough of the physical world to meet her needs, makes us see the "subjective worlds of hallucination, obsession, fever, guilt."[3] Robert Penn Warren, however, notes that Porter's stories are characterized by "rich surface detail scattered with apparently casual profuseness and the close structure which makes such detail meaningful."[4] These two famous comments perceptively pinpoint the central quality of Porter's art—her ability to make mere physical reality resonate with moral significance. By employing a tactic that has dominated modern short fiction since Chekhov, Porter makes her stories (such as her most famous one, "Flowering Judas") seem to be realistic situations in which people are caught in specific moral dilemmas, even as she conveys spiritual allegories in which characters and objects are emblems of universal moral issues.

Although the conflict in "Flowering Judas" takes place, as Welty says about most of Porter's stories, in the interior of the protagonist's life, the story is less a psychological study of one individual's act of renunciation than it is a symbolic story of the basic nature of renunciation. Laura, named perhaps for the unattainable and thus idealistic object of Petrarch's love in his famous sonnets, is caught between her desire to embody her own ideals as a Marxist revolutionary in Mexico and her realization that the very nature of idealism is that it cannot be embodied.

The story opens appropriately with Laura face to face with the revolutionary leader Braggioni, who is so fleshly that his every action compels Laura (and the reader) to confront his bodily being: he sits "heaped" over his guitar, "heaves" himself into song, scratching the instrument as if it were a pet animal, taking the high notes in a "painful squeal." He "bulges" marvelously in his clothes, "swelling" with "ominous ripeness" over his ammunition belt. Porter says that Braggioni has become the symbol of Laura's "many disillusions, for a revolutionist should be lean, animated by heroic faith, a vessel of abstract virtue."[5]

Laura is caught in the disillusionment of all idealists: she feels "betrayed irreparably by the disunion between her way of living and her feeling of what life should be." Externally, she projects the image of one who has rejected the flesh, preferring instead to wear the "uniform of an idea"—blue serge and a nunlike round white collar—and thus nobody touches her, even though they praise her "soft round underlip which promises gaiety yet is always grave." Braggioni tells her that she only thinks she is cold, and he puzzles on the "notorious virginity" of the simple girl who "covers her great round breasts with thick dark cloth and who hides long invaluably beautiful legs under a heavy skirt."

The many dichotomies in the story—Laura's Catholicism and her socialism, her sensuality and her ascetic renunciation, her dedication to the people and her renunciation of genuine involvement—coalesce in the symbolic dichotomy between Braggioni, on the one hand, who affirms life even though it means throwing himself into the physical and becoming a "professional lover of humanity," and Eugenio, on the other, the imprisoned revolutionary who maintains his idealism but negates life and wants to die because he is bored. The key mythic figures who embody this antithesis in the story are Judas, who gives it its title, and Jesus, the one he betrayed.

Given the powerful significance of these dichotomies, it is little wonder that they cannot be solved in actuality, but must instead be resolved aesthetically, in a dream—one that is typical of the medieval dream visions that the story in some ways resembles. In Laura's dream she refuses to follow Eugenio to death because he will not take her hand. In a dream-distorted reversal of the Christian Communion, Eugenio gives her bleeding flowers from the Judas tree (the tree from which Judas hanged himself), which she greedily eats. However, rather than affirming the inextricable union of body and spirit, as does the Christian Communion, Laura's act is a negative one of betrayal for helping Eugenio to escape life. The story ends with the "holy talismanic word" Laura always uses that keeps her from being led into evil but which also keeps her from being involved in life—"No."

William Faulkner and Eudora Welty

William Faulkner's famous story "A Rose for Emily" is less indebted to Chekhovian realism than to the endurance of Poe's

Gothic romanticism. The story is typical of Faulknerian themes and techniques, especially his theme of the decay of the South and his experimentation with viewpoint and narrative time. The story centers on the rejection of time as a linear series of events—both in Emily's efforts to deny death and in Faulkner's refusal to lay out the story in a linear fashion. The central passage occurs near the end, when the narrator describes the old men who come to the funeral who confuse "time with its mathematical progression, as the old do, to whom all the past is not a diminishing road but instead a huge meadow. . . ." This spatialization of time is central to the story, for Emily, much like a character in a story by Poe or Hawthorne, is not so much a real person as an icon, symbolic of an abstraction, a sign frozen in time and space. The clue to her iconic status is that she looks bloated, like a body long submerged in motionless water or else frozen into an idol in the window, a sort of "hereditary obligation upon the town. . . . Dear, inescapable, impervious, tranquil, and perverse." The use of the plural narrator, a kind of choral voice of the town, supplements this notion of time as spatial and Emily as icon, for we do not get the sense of one voice recounting an event laid out neatly in linear time.[6]

It is Eudora Welty, though, who perhaps most clearly exemplifies the strain of writers who, though they have learned the lessons taught by Chekhov, nevertheless align themselves with Isak Dinesen's notion of the mythic divine story. Best known and most discussed for stories that take place in a "season of dreams," in which reality is transformed into fantasy and fable, Welty is a writer who, as Alun R. Jones says, "is conscious of mythical and imaginative reality impinging on and informing the trivial and banal."[7] R. P. Warren has noted in a famous essay that in Welty's stories the logic of things is not the logic of ordinary daylight life, claiming instead that the dreamlike effect of Welty's stories typically results from her ability to squeeze meaning from the most trivial realistic details.

Among all of Eudora Welty's masterly short stories about her profane and holy figures of the American South, perhaps none is so affecting as "Keela, the Outcast Indian Maiden," published in her first collection, *A Curtain of Green* (1941).[8] This little morality play of the clubfooted Negro man made to portray the geek Keela who bites chickens' heads off, and the young barker who seeks to explain his responsibility for the crime, sticks in the reader's memory. However, the cause of the story's impact cannot be attributed solely to the physical horror it depicts. As in any good short story, "Keela" presents a moral dilemma that has the power to involve the reader directly. However, Welty sees more in the case of Little Lee Roy than just one example of man's cruelty to man: he surely caught her imagination as a real-life example of the mythical outcast figure forced to serve as scapegoat for the bestiality of society itself. Like other Welty characters, such as the old, sheeplike women in "A Visit of Charity," Phoenix Jackson in "A Worn Path," and old Solomon in "Livie," he is simple, yet preternaturally wise. His story takes place in the same imaginative and mythical "season of dreams" as the experience of the young deaf boy Joel Mayes in "First Love." Little Lee Roy becomes an inhabitant of that realm of romance that Hawthorne said lay "somewhere between the real word and fairyland" and which Katherine Anne Porter says is Welty's "most familiar territory."[9]

Bernard Malamud

Bernard Malamud's short stories are closer to the oral tradition of folktale than they are to realistic fiction. Although there is much of the Yiddish tale in Malamud's fiction, his short stories also have the tight symbolic structure and ironic and distanced point of view we have come to associate with the short story since Chekhov and Joyce. "The Magic Barrel," the title piece of his 1959 National Book Award winner as well as his most famous story, has often been cited as typical of Malamud's basic narrative technique.[10] Since the story has been said to fluctuate uncertainly between realism and allegory, and to combine the energy of a fairy tale with the tones of a depression moral story, it illustrates as well a basic critical problem in the discrimination of modern short narrative forms.

For example, Earl H. Rovit says that although Malamud's manner is often that of the traditional teller of tales, his poetic and symbolic technique is quite contemporary. The dramatic action of "The Magic Barrel," says Rovit, leads the characters into conflict between the orthodox and the "new" values of Jewish behavior in modern America and fixes that conflict poetically in a final ambiguity: "It is in this sense—a sense in which aesthetic form resolves unresolvable dramatic conflicts—that Malamud departs drastically from the tradition of the Yiddish tale and confronts the demands of modern fictional form."[11]

Many critics have commented on the mysterious tableaulike ending of "The Magic Barrel," noting how what might have been sordid is transformed into something romantic and magical— something in which the two characters exist no longer as real people but, rather, as the essence of lovers in a fairy tale world of pure emblems. Mark Goldman argues that rather than being a realistic dramatic conflict between opposing external forces, the story is a comic fantasy and the conclusion a "consciously ironic parable" in which all the "complex meaning is fixed, flashed back upon the story itself in a kind of Joycean epiphany that runs counter to the neatly packaged endings of the naturalistic tale."[12] Earl Rovit adds that Malamud seems to construct his stories backward, beginning with the final image and then manipulating his characters into dramatic poses that will contribute to the significance of the image; the conflict of the story is resolved by being "fixed poetically" in the final tableau.

These critical comments about "The Magic Barrel"—that it is both realistic and allegorical, naturalistic and fantastic, and that the ambiguity of its narrative form depends to a great extent on a conclusion that resolves dramatic action aesthetically—reflect a basic problem in the nature of the modern short story. The focus on the ending, of course, sounds much like Poe's infamous "Philosophy of Composition," in which he claims to have begun "The Raven" with a final effect and then to have maneuvered everything so as to lead up to it. Moreover, the focus on the ending suggests the characteristic of short fiction already discussed in Joyce's "The Dead," even as the combination of realism and allegory suggests Hawthorne and Poe, and the combination of naturalism and patterning echoes the technique of Chekhov and Hemingway.

As I have tried to show, the short story has from its beginning been a hybrid form combining both the metaphoric mode of the old romance and the metonymic mode of the new realism. Where the novel is primarily a temporal form that creates the illusion of real people existing in a time-bound "as-if-real" world, short fiction, on the contrary, often features characters caught between their "as-if-real" nature and their status as functions of the fable in which they exist. As a result of this dual nature of character in the short story, the form takes on some of the metaphoric qualities that we usually associate with poetry: conflicts are not resolved solely by preestablished plot or by realistic characterization. Instead, as it was in the stories of Hawthorne, Melville, and Poe, characters ultimately confront a metaphoric embodiment of their dilemma—Goodman Brown's forest, Usher's house, Bartleby's wall, and so on. As Rovit, Goldman, and others suggest about "The Magic Barrel," the dramatic conflict of the characters is resolved in a purely metaphoric or aesthetic way.

As a specific form of prose fiction, "The Magic Barrel" is a monostory, in which there is only one "real" character, just as the monodrama is a specific form of drama. With the exception of Leo Finkle, all the other characters are what Northrop Frye has called "stylized figures which expand into psychological archetypes." Although the story opens in a fairy tale manner—"Not long ago there lived in uptown New York, in a small, almost meager room, though crowded with books, Leo Finkle, a rabbinical student"—it soon moves to a realistic level, with the young rabbinical student's practical need for a bride. It quickly becomes clear, however, that a suitable bride (who might enable Finkle to win a congregation) is not what he really needs at all; he needs, rather, something on a deeper level which he has yet to discover consciously. As soon as Finkle summons the matchmaker Pinye Salzman and he suddenly appears one night "out of the dark fourth-floor hallway of the graystone rooming house where Finkle lived," the story moves out of the real world into the interior world of Leo's psyche. And in that world, as Jung points out, reside the primordial images, the archetypes that may be manifested at moments when a new orientation and a new adaptation are necessary.

In such "modern fairy tales" as "The Magic Barrel," every character in the story is a fairy tale agent except the central character. Finkle is presented as if he existed within the realm of actual reality, but Salzman, Salzman's wife, and Stella are all embodiments of primary reality created out of Finkle's own unconscious need. The story of the young rabbi is one that occurs frequently to "as-if-real" characters in short fiction—characters who are either scientists, doctors, lawyers, or preachers, and who by their very being represent the scientific method, the legal method, the logical and the practical mode.

These characters are initially presented as figures who, though confident in their lives, must be confronted by the mythic, primitive realm of being. Classic examples in short fiction are such figures as the narrator in Melville's "Bartleby the Scrivener," who must cope with the "not ordinarily human" Bartleby; the philosopher Joy/Hulga in Flannery O'Connor's "Good Country People," who must confront the primitive figure Manly Pointer; the doctor in William Carlos Williams's "Use of Force," who must confront the savage brat; the scientist in Steinbeck's "The Snake," who must confront the primal woman's association with the chthonic snake; the Reverend Davidson, who must face the primitive atmosphere of Pago Pago in the prostitute Sadie Thompson in Somerset Maugham's story "Rain"; and, of course, Gustave Aschenbach, who must confront the sensuality and decay of Venice and Tadzio in Thomas Mann's "Death in Venice." All these stories—and many more embody this thematic confrontation in nineteenth- and twentieth-century short fiction—present the basic situation of a man or woman confronting the breakup of his or her secure state of being by the disruptive apparition of a Dionysian force, represented as evil, dangerous, supernatural, and primal.

The nature of Finkle's unconscious need is made quite clear by the kind of primordial image he summons. Pinye Salzman, who has been "long in the business" and smells "frankly of fish" seems too extreme to be believed—and indeed he is, if he is perceived as merely a cynical Jewish con man who finally ends up being sold his own bill of goods. However, if we understand him as a mythic figure representative of desires within Finkle's own psyche, then he can be seen as an archetypal structure that, according to Jung, is extremely ancient—the Trickster, who symbolizes the instinctual and irrational, driven by the basic needs of sex and hunger. Salzman's constant hunger for fish is a reflection of Finkle's own hunger for sexuality, but no matter how much Salzman eats, he starves—becoming "transparent to the point of vanishing"—until Finkle finally establishes the level of his real need and accepts the wholly sexual Stella.

As the details of Finkle's particular desires for a wife indicate, the primordial object he seeks is the magic of eroticism; as is usual in the fairy tale, it is sublimated. Stella is surely that archetypal female figure which Jung describes as *anima*. Indeed, the facts that the picture of Stella makes Finkle think of youth and age at the same time, and that she looks as though she is both a suffering victim and an active agent of evil, make clear that Stella is the primordial anima figure. As the conclusion of the story emphasizes, she represents a new life or a rebirth for Finkle, but one that can only follow the death of the old self; it is Finkle for whom Salzman chants.

Finkle's initial impression of Salzman is, as is typical of such *mana* characters, an ambivalent one. Although Salzman has an amiable manner, he has mournful eyes, and he fluctuates throughout between animation and sad repose. Apologizing to Salzman for having called in a matchmaker, Finkle says he thought "it the better part of trial and error—of embarrassing fumbling—to call in an experienced person to advise him on these matters." Since "these matters" have to do with the company of young women, more and more Finkle's embarrassment seems to stem from his calling in Salzman to pimp for him. This is confirmed when it is established that Finkle is not interested in the attributes of Salzman's clients most typical of the marriage broker, nor in their social status, nor in the amount of dowry the father will supply; rather, he is interested in pictures. He wants to know whether or not they are pretty and how old they are. Finkle's real concern is with a young, beautiful virgin. He insists that she be untouched, unspoiled, physically perfect; he wants love and sex, but he wants it to be clean and pure.

Because Salzman has been summoned by Finkle's own primal need, Salzman "knows" what his function is, but he plays an elaborate game to test Finkle's consciously felt reasons for his desire for a bride. When, in the end, Salzman finally relents and grants Stella to him, Finkle correctly has a tormenting suspicion that Salzman had planned all along that this should happen. When Leo tells Salzman that none of his three clients suits him and Salzman asks, "What then suits you?" Leo lets it pass "because he could give only a confused answer." Truly, Leo does not know the answer. What would really suit him is something of which he has no actual experience.

Leo's despair during what he calls the worst week of his life is the result of his realization that he has "involved himself with Salzman without a true knowledge of his own intent." His terrifying insight is that he called in Salzman because he was not capable of finding a bride for himself—an inability related to his realization that, except for his parents, he had "never loved anybody." It now seems to Leo that his "whole life stood starkly revealed and he saw himself for the first time as he truly was— unloved and loveless." The problem here, as it is throughout the story, is that the two kinds of love—divine love and erotic love— are confused in Leo's mind. He never truly disentangles them.

Finkle's discovery of what he really wants—although he still cannot articulate it nor even admit it consciously—occurs when he sees the picture of Stella in the briefcase that stinks of fish. Although after looking at all the pictures he says there is "not a true personality in the lot," we know now that personality is not what he desires. His first view of Stella, who embodies flesh, regardless of all the chivalric overtones of her name (from Sir Philip Sidney's *Astrophel and Stella*), causes him to cry out in final recognition. When Leo runs to Salzman's house, the fact that he could have sworn he had seen Salzman's wife before simply indicates that she too is Salzman. This similarity, and the magic barrel itself, which Leo cannot see in the tenement, he dismisses as figments of his imagination; but they are as real as his previous visions of Salzman's unseen machinations that surround him. For the only reality in the story is the reality of Finkle's need to leave his books in favor of life. Salzman's refusal to grant Stella to Leo, his insistence that it was an accident that the picture was in the briefcase, are all part of Salzman's plan to make Leo himself determine the nature of his physical and emotional needs.

Leo hides under the covers and prays to be rid of Stella— although he actually prays that his prayers to be rid of her are not answered. His final rationalization for his physical desire for her is only that, a rationalization: "He then concluded to convert her to goodness, himself to God. The idea alternately nauseated and exalted him." The tableau or coda of the story sums up and, as Earl Rovit has suggested, resolves the conflict the only way it can be resolved—through metaphor. The elements of the scene—the spring night, Leo carrying a bouquet of violets and rosebuds, Stella smoking under a streetlight, not quite in the red dress and white shoes of the prostitute, her eyes filled with desperate innocence—combine again divine with erotic love. Leo sees in her his redemption from law and from thought and his fall into lawlessness and feeling. Truly Salzman, always smelling of fish, the smell of man's origin in the sea, makes his chant to the dead for Leo Finkle, but it is a death essential to Leo's life.

"The Magic Barrel" is typical of Malamud's short fiction both in its theme and its technique, for it unites tragedy and comedy as well as fantasy and reality. Structured on the pattern of the quest, it makes use of an archetypal figure to examine the identity crisis of a character who fails to see his real self behind his presentational façade. Moreover, it seems a perfect example of what has been referred to by many critics as the formal concentration and symbolic design of Malamud's stories as well as his heavy reliance on a technique of epiphany.[13]

Malamud, probably more than any other contemporary practitioner of the short story form, reminds us that the genre is still closer to the folktale and the romance than it is to the novel form. Its contents are more mythic and emotional than they are realistic and ideological. In Malamud, one can perceive the entire range of the short story genre, from the romantic tales of Hawthorne to the objective and ironic dramas of Chekhov; from the lyric narratives of Turgenev to the grotesque moral dilemmas of Flannery O'Connor. Although Malamud has written very little about his fiction, he has affirmed his conviction that the short story demands form above all, and that although he supports literary freedom, such freedom does not necessarily lead to art. Malamud asserts the importance of tradition, for it is only within the conventions of art, he believes, that art can be expressed: "The best endures in the accomplishment of the masters. One will be convinced, if he or she reads conscientiously and widely, that form as ultimate necessity is the basis of literature."[14] Malamud says he loves the pleasures of the short story, not only because of what he calls the "fast payoff" but also because the short story "packs a self in a few pages predicating a lifetime."

John Steinbeck

The combination of reality and fantasy in which a realistic character confronts the embodiment of a *mana* figure can also be seen in the stories of Truman Capote, Flannery O'Connor, Carson

McCullers, and John Steinbeck. In "The Snake," a typical story from his collection *The Long Valley*, Steinbeck presents the tension between the life of science and reason, on the one hand, and the mythic world of primal reality, on the other.[15] The forces that oppose each other in Steinbeck's story are suggested in the first paragraph by the juxtaposition of the laboratory and the tide pool: the one closed off from nature yet built for the purpose of observing nature, the other the primal source of life itself where the mysteries of nature truly take place. The action that opens the story—Dr. Phillips's leaving the tide pool for the laboratory—creates an atmosphere that resonates with ominousness. Even when we discover that the clammy sack is filled only with common starfish, and that the dissection table is used for small animals, we are still apprehensive that there is something "unnatural" about the laboratory. This is more or less confirmed when we are told that the young doctor has the "preoccupied eyes of one who looks through a microscope a great deal" and his bedroom is a book-lined cell containing an army cot, a reading light, and an uncomfortable chair. The imagery with which he is described is too much that of one who, having withdrawn from life, is content merely to look on—one who does not live life but experiments with it.

Most of the description of the mysterious woman who enters his lab to buy a snake clearly and simply establishes her physical identity with the snake. Tall and lean, dressed in a severe dark suit, she has straight black hair growing low on a flat forehead. "He noted how short her chin was between lower lip and point." As she waits to talk to him, she seems completely at rest. "Her eyes were bright but the rest of her was almost in a state of suspended animation. He thought, 'Low metabolic rate, almost as low as a frog's, from the looks.'" However, other details and actions of the woman are not so clearly related to the snake. When the doctor goes over to the rattlesnake cage, he turns to find her standing beside him. "He had not heard her get up from the chair. He had heard only the splash of water among the piles and the scampering of rats on the wire screen." Later, when the doctor puts the rat into the snake cage, the room becomes very silent. "Dr. Phillips did not know whether the water sighed among the piles or whether the woman sighed." Finally, when the woman leaves, the doctor hears her footsteps on the stairs but "could not hear her walk away on the pavement." These details identify the woman not so much with the snake as with the sea itself: the connection of the sounds she makes with the sound of the waves underneath the laboratory makes this clear. The doctor does not hear her walk away on the pavement because she does not walk away: she goes back to the tide pool from whence she came, back to the "deep pool of consciousness" out of which she awakens when the doctor is ready to talk to her. She does not wish to look into the microscope because, being a mythic creature, her vision sees not narrowly but in a large circle that is all-encompassing. Most helpful in understanding the nature and origin of the woman in the story are Steinbeck's tentative notions of a racial unconscious developed in *The Log from the Sea of Cortez*: developing the analogy between the sea as primal source of man and source of the dream symbols of man's unconsciousness, Steinbeck gives us a basis for understanding that the strange woman in "The Snake" comes from the tide pool of the sea even as she comes from the unconscious of the young doctor and, ultimately, of all men.

To understand why the snake-woman or instinctual force has risen abruptly from the doctor's unconscious to confront him, we need not try to understand the "personal" contents of his unconscious any more than we need to try to understand or postulate a particular sexual neurosis for the woman. Indeed, the story gives us no basis for trying to understand either as individual characters. The doctor, embodying as he does a scientific and therefore detached existence, is simply intolerable in his one-sidedness. The woman, on the other hand, is a force that the doctor finds threatening, because he refuses to recognize and integrate the archetypal contents of his unconscious which she embodies.

After the woman leaves, the doctor sits in front of the snake cage and tries to "comb out his thought"; but the only explanation he has, and perhaps the only explanation possible is, "Maybe I'm too much alone." Indeed, the doctor has been visited by the mythic force because he is alone. Cut off from life by his sole attention to the observation of life, cut off from any spiritual realm by his concern for the scientific, the doctor remains outside that "solidarity of life" which ultimately is religious. Perhaps realizing this, yet helpless to do anything about it, the doctor admits, "If I knew—no, I can't pray to anything."

John Cheever

John Cheever presents yet another clear example of the combination of fantasy and post-Chekhovian realism which characterizes the modern short story. Whereas his best-known early stories, "Torch Song" and "The Enormous Radio," are outright fantasies, later stories, such as "O Youth and Beauty" and "The Country Husband," are more realistic treatments of middle-aged men trying to hold on to youth and some meaningful place in life. "The Swimmer" combines both most clearly.[16]

The basic problem in "The Swimmer" is determining the nature of the reality of the events at any given point in the story. As suggested by Hal Blythe and Charlie Sweet, the reader must decide if the first part, as Neddy thinks of earlier and happier times, is fantasy, or if the last part is a fantastic future that Neddy projects as he waits in the gazebo for the storm to pass. The distortion of time is suggested by several things: a tree that is losing its leaves in summer, Neddy's wondering if his memory is failing him, references to misfortunes he seems to know nothing about, his loss of weight which makes his trunks feel loose, and his increasing sense of fatigue and age. This story is a reversal in some ways of Ambrose Bierce's experimentation with the distortion of time in "An Occurrence at Owl Creek Bridge": where in Bierce's story a short period of "real time" seems to be unnaturally lengthened, in Cheever's fantasy, a long period of "real time" seems unnaturally foreshortened. In Bierce's story the central character must be convinced that what he thinks is happening is "really happening," whereas in Cheever's story the central character must be allowed to believe that his metaphoric swim through (depending on one's perspective) future or past time is actually a swim in present time through space.

The metaphoric nature of the swim is suggested at various points in the story. For example, the idea that he is an explorer or a legendary figure, prepares the reader for the tragic nature of his experience; the fact that he thinks of the pool as a river suggests the conventional fabulistic metaphor of "the river of life"; and the fact that near the end of the story he feels he has been "immersed too long" suggests a basic flaw in his character—his self-centered desire that time stand still.

Susan Glaspell and Charlotte Gilman

The women's movement and the growth of women's studies departments in universities have expanded the short story canon by reviving interest in stories written by women. In addition to the "rediscovery" of Kate Chopin, Sara Orne Jewett, Edith Wharton, and Willa Cather—writers who are known primarily for their novels—perhaps the best-known of these revivals in the realm of the short story are Susan Glaspell's "A Jury of Her Peers" and Charlotte Gilman's "The Yellow Wallpaper," both published early in the century but only widely anthologized in textbooks in the late 1970s and early 1980s.

Because "A Jury of Her Peers," published in 1917, makes use of detective-story conventions developed by Poe to present its feminist theme, its structure self-reflexively parallels the reader's unravelling of the mystery of motivation at the heart of the story. The women, based on their identification with the accused, discover details—spilled sugar, awkward stitches in a quilt, an empty bird cage—that they determine to be clues. The men, on the other hand, think these are merely trifles. This difference, between meaningless details and meaningful ones, is an important distinction for the short story form, especially in the twentieth century; as we have seen, since Chekhov and Joyce, the short story derives meaning from the transformation of seemingly trivial details into meaningful details because of the role they play in the contextual mystery of motivation. The attorney makes the problem explicitly clear near the end of the story: "If there was some definite thing—something to show. Something to make a story about. A thing that would connect up with this clumsy way of doing it." And this, indeed, is the problem the reader always faces—how to interpret all the details, determine which are thematically relevant and which are motivated primarily by verisimilitude, and then rearrange them in a new meaningful way so that the motive for the mystery can be laid bare.

Like "A Jury of Her Peers," "The Yellow Wallpaper," published in 1892, has been anthologized and widely read only recently because of its thematic relevance to the rise in academic feminism in American universities. The story employs an interesting use of the technique of first-person point of view and the relationship between writing and reality—especially the difference between traditional masculine and feminine texts. The story makes use of a common convention of Gothic romance, which has often been interpreted as women's fiction. The primary convention the story uses is the traditional difference between how men and women supposedly approach reality: the husband, who is a doctor or scientist, has no patience with faith, superstition, or anything that cannot be physically verified and converted into mathematical figures, in contrast with the wife's imaginative power and her "habit of story-making."

Serving as a background to this tension is the wallpaper itself, which gives the story its title: although it serves as an image of domestic "woman's things," it takes on significance because of the nature of the "patterns" it embodies. What the narrator does is to transform a "pointless pattern" into a meaningful one by following it to its conclusion or end and thus determining its purpose. Of course, as the story proceeds and the doctor's wife perceives or projects a woman behind the pattern, the reader knows that inevitably the woman must be herself, for the conventional rule that applies here is that if one projects a pattern, the pattern then indeed reflects the self. The story thus involves two basic notions of patterns that the reader may need to unravel—patterns created by society itself, which entrap a woman and bind her, and patterns the mind of the woman herself creates, which follow only the law of her own psychic distress.

Chapter 5

Contemporary Renaissance

Although the term postmodernism is difficult to define, most critics seem to agree that if a major part of modernism in the early part of the century was manifested as James Joyce's frustration of conventional expectations about the cause-and-effect nature of plot and the "as-if-real" nature of character, then postmodernism pushes this tendency even further, so that contemporary fiction is less and less about objective reality and more and more about its own creative processes. According to the basic paradigm that underlies this movement—grounded in European phenomenology and structuralism—"everyday reality" itself is the result of a fiction-making process, whereby new data are selectively accepted and metaphorically transformed to fit pre-existing schemas and categories. One critical implication of this theory is that literary fictions constitute a highly concentrated and accessible analogue of the means by which people create that diffuse and invisible reality that they take for granted as the everyday.

The primary effect of this mode of thought on contemporary fiction is that the short story has a tendency to loosen its illusion of reality in order to explore the reality of its illusion.

Rather than presenting itself "as if" it were real—a mimetic mirroring of external reality—postmodernist short fiction often makes its own artistic conventions and devices the subject of the story as well as its theme. The underlying assumption is that the forms of art are explicable by the laws of art; literary language is not a proxy for something else but, rather, an object of study itself. William H. Gass notes that the fiction writer now better understands his medium; he is "ceasing to pretend that his business is to render the world; he knows, more often now, that his business is to make one, and to make one from the only medium of which he is master—language."[1] The short story as a genre has always been more likely to lay bare its fictionality than the novel, which, with the exception of "experimental" novels, has traditionally tried to cover it up. Fictional self-consciousness in the short story does not allow the reader to maintain the comfortable assumption that what is depicted is real; instead, the reader is made uncomfortably aware that the only reality is the depiction itself—the language act of the fiction-making process.

Jorge Luis Borges

The most important precursor of the contemporary self-reflexive short story is the South American writer Jorge Luis Borges, who in turn owes his own allegiance to Poe and Kafka. Borges might well be called a writer's writer, for the subject of his stories is more often the nature of writing itself than actual events in the world. Because of Borges's overriding interest in aesthetic and metaphysical reality, his stories, like many of those of Poe, often resemble fables or essays.

One of his best-known essay/stories, "Pierre Menard, Author of the Quixote," deals with a French writer who decides to invent the *Quixote*, in spite of the fact that it has already been written by Cervantes. Borges's narrator then compares the two versions and finds them identical; however, he argues that the second version is richer, more ambitious, and in many ways more subtle than Cervantes's original. In another well-known story, "Funes the Memorious," Borges presents a character who is unable to forget details of his experience, no matter how small.

If the situations of these two men seem alien to ordinary human experience, it is because Borges is interested in the extraordinary nature of metaphysical rather than physical reality. The fact that Pierre Menard can write a *Quixote* identical to the original yet create a more complex and subtle work can be attributed to the notion that one reads a present work with all previous works inscribed within it. The fact that Funes is condemned to remember every single detail of his experience means that he can never tell stories because he is unable to select or abstract from his experience.

Borges is also particularly interested in human reality as the result of language and game, as well as the result of the projection of the mind itself. "Tlön, Uqbar, Orbis Tertius" explores the intellectual productions of an imaginary planet; "The Library of Babel" deals with the inhabitants of a library, infinite in its circular and cyclical structure, that records everything that has happened, will happen, or might happen; "The Lottery in Babylon" features a lottery that transforms all reality itself into chance. Borges's most common technique is to parody previously established genres such as the science fiction story, the philosophical essay, or the detective story by pushing them to absurd extremes. He realizes that reality is not the composite of the simple empirical data that we experience every day but, rather, is much more subjective, metaphysical, and thus mysterious than we often think it to be. Poe's detective story reminds us, says Borges, that reality is a highly patterned human construct, like fiction itself.

John Barth

Although John Barth's late 1960s essay "The Literature of Exhaustion" has been much misunderstood to have argued that contemporary fiction writers have "run out" of a subject for their work, it actually urges more of the kind of self-conscious experimentation being practiced by Borges. At the same time, Barth temporarily turned from the novel form to the short story, publishing *Lost in the Funhouse*, an experimental collection in which the stories refused to focus their attention on their so-called proper subject— the external world—and instead continually turned the reader's attention back to what Barth considered their real subject—the process of fiction-making.

Barth's approach to fiction has been summed up quite pointedly in the essays that appear in his collection of occasional pieces entitled *The Friday Book*.[2] Barth insists that the prosaic in fiction is there only to be transformed into fabulation. The artist's ostensible subject is not the main point; rather, it is only an excuse or raw material for focusing on the nature of the fiction-making process. For Barth, the fiction writer is like God, for the universe itself is a fiction. Although this focus is as old as the metaphysical and aesthetic views of Edgar Allan Poe (to whom Barth frequently pays tribute), Barth makes it his own with a vengeance. For Barth, the first requirement of the fiction writer is the ability to tell a story, but to tell a story in such a way that by the very act of telling the story inevitably turns back on itself to focus on process rather than simple mimetic product. Barth agrees with Thomas Mann that what the artist talks about is never the main point, that it is, rather, only the raw material for focusing on the fiction-making itself. Great literature, says Barth, regardless of what it is about, is almost always about itself as well. The fantasy we call "reality" and the fantasy we call "fantasy" are only matters of cultural consensus; the focus in both is always on "as if."

"Autobiography" is one of the most thoroughgoing self-reflexive fictions in *Lost in the Funhouse*, for it does not pretend, as conventional fictions do, that the voice that speaks the fiction is the voice of a human being; rather, it confronts directly the inescapable fact that what speaks to us is the story itself—thus, the only autobiography a story can present is a story of its own coming into being and its own mode of existence.[3] Every statement in "Autobiography" is an assertion, in one way or another, about this particular fiction's fictionality, one whose mother was a mere fictional device of self-reflexivity which the father/author was attracted to one day. Some of the key characteristics of fiction in general that the story foregrounds are these: fictions have no life unless they are read; fictions cannot know themselves; fictions have no body; fictions have one-track minds; fictions can neither start themselves nor stop themselves; fictions reflect their authors in distorted ways.

Donald Barthelme

Donald Barthelme is the most influential postmodernist writer to specialize in the short story. Ever since his first story appeared in the *New Yorker* in 1963 and his first collection of stories *Come Back, Dr. Caligari* appeared in 1964, many critics have complained that his work is without subject matter, without character, without plot, and without concern for the reader's understanding. These very characteristics, of course, have placed Barthelme with such writers as Robert Coover, William H. Gass, Ronald Sukenick, Raymond Federman, John Hawkes, and John Barth as the leading practitioners of postmodernist fiction.

For Barthelme, the problem of language is the problem of reality, for reality, he implies, is the result of language processes. The problem of words, Barthelme realizes, is that so much contemporary language is used up, has become trash, dreck. Barthelme takes as his primary task the recycling of language, making metaphor out of the castoffs of technological culture. For Barthelme, as for the poet always, the task is to try to reach, through metaphor, and the resulting defamiliarization, that ineffable realm of knowledge which Barthelme says lies somewhere between mathematics and religion "in which what may fairly be called truth exists."

It is, however, the extreme means by which Barthelme attempts to reach this truth that makes his fiction so difficult. Barthelme has noted that if photography forced painters to reinvent painting, then films have forced fiction writers to reinvent fiction. Since films tell a realistic narrative so well, the fiction writer must develop a new principle. Collage, says Barthelme, is the central principle of all art in the twentieth century: its point is that "unlike things are stuck together to make, in the best case, a new reality. This new reality, in the best case, may be or imply a comment on the other realities from which it came, and may also be much else. It's an itself, if it's successful."[4] One of the implications of this collage process is a radical shift from the usual temporal, cause-and-effect process of fiction to the more spatial and metaphoric process of poetry.

The most basic example of Barthelme's use of this mode is his popular story, "The Balloon," the premise of which is that a large balloon has encompassed the city. The narrator of the story says that it is wrong to speak of "situations, implying sets of circumstances leading to some resolution, some escape of tension."[5] In this story there are no situations—only the balloon, a concrete particular thing to which people react and which they try to explain. Although we discover at the end that the balloon is the objectification of something personal to the speaker, we realize that because the speaker's feelings must be objectified in images and language, the balloon is removed from life and cut free of any unambiguous referential meaning. The participant or viewer then becomes a co-artist who helps to construct or manipulate whatever responses the balloon elicits. The balloon is an extended metaphor for the Barthelme story itself, to which people try to find some means of access, and which creates varied critical responses and opinions.

To plunge into a Barthelme story is to immerse oneself in the flotsam and jetsam of contemporary society, for his stories are not so much plotted tales as they are parodies and satires based on the public junk and commercial media hype that clutter up and cover over our private lives. Because they are satires, many of the stories are based not on the lives of individuals but on the means by which that abstraction called "society" or "the public" is manipulated. Barthelme is not really interested in the personal lives of his characters; in fact, few seem to have personal lives. Rather, he wishes to present modern men and women as the products of the media and the language that surround them. Furthermore, he is not so much interested in an art that serves merely to reflect or imitate the world outside itself; instead, he is concerned to create artworks that are interesting in and for themselves. The basic fictional issue overshadowing his work is that if reality is itself a process of fictional creation by metaphor-making humans, then the modern writer who wishes to write about reality can only write truthfully about that very process. To write only about this process, however, is to run the risk of dealing with language on a level that leaves the reader gasping for something tangible and real, even if that reality is only an illusion. In one of his most autobiographical stories, "See the Moon," the persona says, "Fragments are the only forms I trust." And he has a wall filled with fragments that he hopes will one day merge, blur, and cohere into something meaningful. In "The Indian Uprising," the narrator desires "strings of language" that extend in every direction to "bind the world into a rushing, ribald whole."

The central problem of Barthelme's use of irony and parody—in which one parodies oneself and therefore asserts nothing—is best summed up in his story "Kierkegaard Unfair to Schlegel." The persona reminds us of Søren Kierkegaard's belief that the effect of irony is to deprive the object of its reality. The limitation of the ironist, says Kierkegaard, is that the actuality created by the ironist is a comment on a former actuality rather than a new actuality. Although Barthelme says that collage is not simply a comment on the old object but rather the creation of a new one, he is obviously not unaware of Kierkegaard's warning.

This problem is also the central focus of Barthleme's "Me and Mrs. Mandible" in which a thirty-five-year-old man is mistakenly taken to be an eleven-year-old boy. The cause of his problem—and indeed the original source of all of Barthelme's stories—is the narrator's realization that although people "read signs as promises," the truth is that "signs are signs and some of them are lies." In a world in which one cannot take signs as promises, all the props are kicked out from under one and all the old, comfortable assumptions are destroyed.

The short story seems clearly to be a more appropriate vehicle for Barthelme's vision than the novel, for the short story has always been less bound to the convention of realism than the novel. The modern short story has also been more closely aligned with the spatial techniques of poetry than the novel. Perhaps the best definition of Barthelme's view of the short story can be found in one of his best-known stories, "Robert Kennedy Saved from Drowning." In this parody of pop journalism style, which satirizes nonfiction's pretensions to truth, Robert Kennedy quotes the French writer Georges Poulet, who talked about "recognizing in the instant which lives and dies, which surges out of nothingness and which ends in dreams, an intensity and depth of significance which ordinarily attaches only to the whole of existence." Barthelme's fiction continually blurs the lines between fiction and an analytical discourse about fiction, for his stories, by disavowing that the function of fiction is a mimetic mirroring of reality, throw into question accepted definitions of reality itself.

Charles Baxter, John L'Heureux, T. Coraghessan Boyle

More recent practitioners of the fantastic fiction of Borges, Barth, and Barthelme are Charles Baxter, John L'Heureux, and T. Coraghessan Boyle. Baxter's story "The Cliff" is a typical post-modernist fable combining realistic characters and a realistic setting with the kind of fantastic event we associate with mythic stories. Like the "magical realism" stories of Julio Cortázar and Gabriel García Márquez, "The Cliff," both in its language and its characterization, pushes this twentieth-century trend to combine the realistic and the fantastic to extremes. The story takes an earthly approach to a most basic human desire—to escape gravity and fly. Although the old man in the story says the boy must keep his body pure for "the stuff" the two of them are doing, he himself smokes and drinks, admitting the inevitability of his loss of righteousness. The magic of the boy's flight stems from the phrase—"whatever he thought, he did," for it expresses the ultimate desire of the mythical Icarus—to transcend earthly limitations by transforming wish into act.

John L'Heureux's Kafkaesque parable "The Anatomy of Desire" suggests that the basic human condition is the need to lose the self in the other, to be completely possessed. When Hanley, the protagonist, who has been tortured by having all his skin removed, tells the nurse (called "the saint") that he wants to be inside her, and they make love, he says intercourse is only a metaphor for what he wants. When he puts on her skin to be "inside her," this too is only a metaphor, and he realizes that one can never possess the other—one can only desire. The story of the general who tortured him runs parallel to the story of Hanley, for his love for Hanley means that he has reached the state that Hanley desires—to be completely possessed. However, to be possessed is to be tormented with desire, for the general's emotional sense of possession is only a metaphor as well.

T. Coraghessan Boyle's most pervasive fictional theme is the importance of history; his most predominant fictional method is satire. Many of his stories, although they usually satirize the phenomena of popular culture, depend on historical events or characters. Boyle's first collection, *Descent of Man*, features such absurd situations as the movie star dog Lassie leaving his master Timmy for a love affair with a coyote, and a woman falling in love with a brilliant chimpanzee who is translating Darwin and Nietzsche into "Yerkish." Boyle continues this kind of absurdist satire and parody in his second collection, *Greasy Lake and Other Stories*, but some of the stories in this collection achieve such a powerful significance that they go beyond simple satire. Although the collection contains parodies of Sherlock Holmes and Gogol's famous story "The Overcoat," as well as absurd situations—for example, a secret love affair between Dwight Eisenhower and the wife of Nikita Khrushchev—it also contains such surrealistically sublime pieces as "The Hector Quesadilla Story" about a baseball game that goes on forever and classic tragicomic nightmares, such as "Greasy Lake."

"Greasy Lake" is a realistic yet surrealistic story about the posturing efforts of young men wanting to be tough. Boyle has said that the story is about strutting around thinking you are "bad," only to find someone tougher than you are. The story raises a fundamental question, says Boyle: Where is the bottom, and do you really want to get there? The metaphor for the bottom is the Greasy Lake itself, the ultimate end of the basic ironic dichotomy in the story, between clean-cut suburbanism and greasy primitivism. Although there is a distinction between the pretense of danger and real danger, the story suggests that the pretense can itself be dangerous. The progression from comic posturing and slapstick comedy to Gothic horror and final bathos is handled so deftly that the reader is irresistibly carried along with it.

Raymond Carver

Alongside this extension of the Poelike or Kafkaesque fantastic story is a further development of the Chekhovian-Joycean realistic story, the most polished and profound practitioner of which is Raymond Carver. Since his first collection of short stories, *Will You Please Be Quiet, Please?*, was nominated for the National Book Award in 1976, Carver has perhaps been the most critically admired short story writer in contemporary American literature. Carver has been the leader of a revival of interest in the short story in the late 1970s and early 1980s, part of a trend of short fiction that author John Barth playfully termed "hyperrealistic minimalism," or the "less-is-more" school. Carver's stories are stubbornly taciturn; like the stories of Anton Chekhov and Ernest Hemingway, they communicate by indirection, suggesting much by saying little. The stories are like stark black-and-white snapshots of lives lived in a kind of quiet, even silent, desperation, and they are told in a language that, even as it seems simple and straightforward, is quite studied and stylized.

"Neighbors," one of Carver's most puzzling and shocking stories, focuses on Bill and Arlene Miller, a young couple who feels that the lives of their neighbors Harriet and Jim Stone are somehow brighter and fuller than their own. The story begins when the Stones go on a trip and ask the Millers to look after their apartment and to water the plants. However, Bill's routine visits to the apartment arouse him sexually; he begins to stay longer and longer in the apartment each time, taking trivial things—such as a container of pills and cigarettes—and nibbling food from the refrigerator. His fascination with the apartment becomes more bizarre when he secretly takes off from work and slips in to spend the day alone there. He first tries on a shirt and Bermuda shorts belonging to Jim Stone, and then a brassiere and pair of panties belonging to Harriet. The story comes to a climax that evening when his wife goes over to the apartment and the reader discovers that she is similarly fascinated, telling her husband she found some pictures in a drawer; although we are not told what kind of pictures they are, we may assume they depict the secret sexual life of the Stones. When the couple goes back across the hall to their own apartment, they consider that maybe the Stones won't come back; and when they discover that they have locked the key to the apartment inside, they feel desperate. "'Don't worry,' he said into her ear. 'For God's sake, don't worry.' They stayed there. They held each other. They leaned into the door as if against a wind and braced themselves."

Typical of Carver's early work, the story offers no explanation for the fascination the apartment holds for the young couple; the closest Carver will come to an explanation is the girl saying "It's funny . . . to go in someone's place like that," to which her husband replies "It *is* funny." However, this is not a story about a sexually perverted couple; rather, it is a story about the fascination of visiting someone else's secret inner reality and of the excitement of temporarily taking on their identity. To enter into the dark and hidden world of the "neighbors" is to experience a voyeuristic thrill. The dissatisfaction that everyone feels at times with being merely him- or herself and no one else, and the universal desire to change places with someone else, is delicately handled here. For example, Bill's fantasy of changing places with his neighbor is suggested by the simple act of his looking into the bathroom mirror, closing his eyes and then looking again—as if by that blink a transformation could take place. Moreover, the fact that Bill wants to make love to his wife after visiting the apartment reflects the erotic thrill of peeking into the life of someone else and then, almost in an act of autoeroticism, fulfilling that fantasy with whoever is at hand. The desperation the couple feels at the end, as they find themselves locked out of the apartment, bracing themselves as if against a wind, points to the impossibility of truly entering into the lives of others, except to visit and to violate.

"Why Don't You Dance?," the first story in Carver's controversial second collection *What We Talk About When We Talk About Love*, is characteristic of the qualities of his short fiction at the high point of his career.[7] The story begins with an unidentified man who has, for some unexplained reason, put all his furniture out on his front lawn. What makes the event more than just a mundane yard sale is the fact that the man has arranged the furniture just as it was when it was in the house; he has even plugged in the television and other appliances so that they work just as they did inside. The only mention of the man's wife is the fact that the bed has a nightstand and a reading lamp on his side of the bed and a nightstand and reading lamp on "her" side of the bed; this is Carver's typically understated way of suggesting that the man's marriage has collapsed and that his wife is no longer around.

The story begins its muted dramatic turn when a young couple who is furnishing their first apartment stop by and begin to inspect the furniture. As the young woman tries out the bed and the young man turns on the television, their dialogue is clipped and cryptic, reminiscent of the dialogue of characters in a story by Ernest Hemingway. When the man returns from a trip to the store, the dialogue continues in its understated and laconic way, as the couple makes offers for some of the furnishings, and the man indifferently accepts whatever they offer. When the man plays a record on the phonograph, the young man and woman, then the older man and woman, begin to dance. The story ends with a brief epilogue, weeks later, when the girl is telling a friend about the incident. The story ends with the lines: "She kept talking. She told everyone. There was more to it, and she was trying to get it talked out. After a time, she quit trying."

"Why Don't You Dance?" is an embodiment of the way that modern short fiction since Chekhov has sought to embody inner reality by means of simple descriptions of outer reality. By placing all his furniture on his front lawn, the man has externalized what has previously been hidden inside the house. When the young couple arrives, they metaphorically replace the older man's lost relationship with their new one, creating their own relationship on the remains of the man's. However, the story is not a hopeful one, for the seemingly minor conflicts revealed by the dialogue between the two young people—his watching television and her wanting him to try the bed, or her wanting to dance and his drinking—presage another doomed relationship like the one the older man had. Indeed, there is more to it, as the young woman senses, but she cannot quite articulate the meaning of the event; she can only, as storytellers must, retell it over and over again, trying to get it talked out and thereby understand it intuitively.

The lyricism of Carver's style lies in a "will to style" in which reality is stripped of its physicality and exists only in the hard, bare outlines of the event. Most of Carver's stories have the ambience more of dream than of everyday reality, yet the stories are not parables in the usual sense. His characters give us the feel of emotional reality which reaches the level of myth, even as they refuse to give us the feel of physical or simple psychological reality. The most basic theme of Carver's stories is the tenuous union between men and women and the mysterious separations that always seem imminent.

Carver abruptly changed both his characteristic style and his typical theme in the middle of his career. The stories that appear in his last two collections, *Cathedral* and *Where I'm Calling From*, are more optimistic and hopeful than the earlier stories; they also are more voluble and detailed, exhibiting an increasing willingness by Carver and his narrators to discuss, explain, and explore the emotions and situations that give rise to the stories. Instead of separation, Carver's later stories move toward union or reunion.

They are characterized by a mood of reconciliation and calm self-knowledge and acceptance. Although this shift in moral perspective moves Carver's fiction toward a more conventional short story form, all of his stories are told in such a way that the universal human mystery of union and separation is exposed, even if it is not always explained. The simple, yet complex, humanity that Carver reveals can neither be understood nor cured by the pop psychology of modern life; as in the great short stories of his predecessors, it can only be captured in the pure and painful events of human beings who mysteriously come together and come apart.

"Cathedral," the title story of Carver's third collection, is typical of the ways in which his technique and thematic concerns changed after his own personal life became more stable.[8] The story contains much more exposition and discussion, more background and efforts at clarification, than do the stories in Carver's first two cryptic collections. "Cathedral" is narrated in the first person by a young man who resents the visit of his wife's old friend, a blind man for whom the wife once read. Unlike Carver's earlier stories, which focus primarily on the immediate situation detached from its background, the first quarter of "Cathedral" recounts the narrator's knowledge of his wife's previous married life, her friendship with the blind man—especially the fact that they have sent audiotapes back and forth to each other—and even the blind man's wife Beulah, who has just died. Although the relevance of all this information to the final epiphanic revelation of the story is never made clear, it does reveal the cynicism of the narrator, who obviously resents his wife's relationship with the blind man. It also reveals him as an insensitive character who has prejudiced notions about a variety of subjects; for example, his only notion of blind people comes from the movies, and he asks if the blind man's wife was "a Negro" just because her name is Beulah.

The conversation between the narrator, his wife, and the blind man, which makes up the center of the story, is inconclusive; for the most part it is devoted to the blind man's dispelling many of the prejudiced expectations the narrator has about the blind. The climax toward which the story inevitably moves—a confrontation between the narrator and the blind man—begins when the wife goes to sleep, and the two men drink and smoke marijuana together. The encounter is brought about by a program on television about the Church in the Middle Ages, which the narrator watches because there is nothing else on television. When the program features a cathedral, the narrator asks the blind man if he knows what a cathedral is. The blind man says he has no real idea and asks the narrator to describe a cathedral to him. When the narrator fails, the blind man asks him if he is religious, to which the narrator says he does not believe in anything.

The blind man then asks the narrator to find some paper and a pen so that they can draw a cathedral together. The blind man puts his hand over the hand of the narrator and tells him to draw, so that the blind man's hand can follow the lines. As they continue to draw, the blind man asks the narrator to close his eyes. When they finish, the blind man asks him to look at the drawing and tell him what he thinks. But the narrator keeps his eyes closed. He knows that he is in his house, but he says he didn't feel like he was inside anything. His final statement is typical of Carver inconclusiveness: "It's really something."

"Cathedral," a much-admired Carver story, often finds its way into literature anthologies for college classes, even though it is less experimental and innovative, more explicit and more conventionally optimistic and moral, than are his earlier stories. Obviously, the narrator has reached some sort of traditional epiphany at the end; ironically, whereas he has been morally blind before, now he is able to see. The story is about his ultimate ability to identify with the blind man, about the two men blending together into one entity. The narrator's experience is a spiritual experience in the broadest sense; the fact that a cathedral brings the two men together makes that clear enough. The story involves far more dialogue than do Carver's earlier stories, in great part because it is a first-person narrative in which the personality of the narrator lies at the thematic heart of the story itself—but also because Carver seems to feel he has an explanation for things he did not try to account for previously. It is a tendency toward explanation that has moved his later work closer to the kind of moral fiction of which his early teacher John Gardner would have approved.

This shift in Carver's art can also be seen in his revision of some of his earlier stories, the most striking of which is his transformation of an early story "The Bath" in a later one he has renamed "A Small Good Thing."[9] Both stories focus on a couple whose son is hit by a car on his eighth birthday, and who lies comatose in a hospital. This horrifying event is made more intolerable when the couple receive annoying anonymous phone calls from a baker from whom the wife had earlier ordered a custom-made birthday cake. "The Bath" is a brief story, told in Carver's early, neutralized style. "A Small Good Thing," five times longer than "The Bath," develops the emotional life of the couple in more sympathetic detail, suggesting that their prayers for their son bind them together in a genuine human communion they have never felt before. But the most radical difference in the revision is in the conclusion: where in the first version the child's death abruptly ends the story, in the second, the couple visits the baker after the boy's death. He shares their sorrow; they share his loneliness, and the story ends in reconciliation.

"The Bath" is a story about the mysterious disruption of human life, but "A Small, Good Thing" is a story that moves toward a more conventionally moral ending—acceptance. The image of the parents in the warm, sweet-smelling bakery, momentarily reconciled by their sense of communion with the baker, is a clear image of Carver's moral shift from the skeptical to the affirmative, from the sense of the unspeakable mystery of human life to the sense of how simple and moral life is after all.

Raymond Carver is perhaps the most important figure in the renaissance of short fiction sparked in American literature in the 1980s. He belongs in a line of short story writers that begins with Anton Chekhov and progresses through such masters of the form as Sherwood Anderson, Katherine Anne Porter, Ernest Hemingway, and Bernard Malamud. On the basis of a small output of stories, Carver seems likely to remain a significant figure in the history of modern American literature. His understanding of the merits of the short story form, as well as his sensitivity to the situation of modern men and women caught in tenuous relationships and inexplicable separations, has made him a spokesman for those who cannot articulate their own dilemmas. Although critics are divided over the relative merits of Carver's early, bleak experimental stories and his later more conventional and morally optimistic stories, few dispute that Raymond Carver is a modern master of the "much-in-little" nature of the Chekhovian short story form.

Tobias Wolff, Ann Beattie, Mary Robison

A number of other contemporary short story writers are currently practicing a form of the Chekhovian-Joycean mode of modern realism. The stories of Tobias Wolff are much like those of Raymond Carver. "Say Yes" is typical.[10] The initiating situation is trivial and domestic, and the characters, ordinary people who are not particularly articulate, exist only to present the viewpoints central to the conflict in the story; we know very little about them otherwise. As is often the case in Carver stories too, this simple situation soon develops into a significant and universal conflict for no other reason than the fact that the participants are a husband and wife and, therefore, by the very tenuousness of their relationship, are always hovering on the edge of conflict and collapse. In fact, Wolff's story, by using the metaphor of racial difference, focuses on the basic difference between all human beings, especially men and women, husbands and wives.

The issue that precipitates the conflict—whether white people should marry black people—begins casually; for the man it seems to have nothing to do with himself personally. However, as soon as he says that people of different races could never really know each other and the wife asks, "Like you know me?" the issue becomes personalized. The one thing we recognize about the husband is that he is confident of his own point of view; it is his cocky self-assurance that moves the story forward. The difference between the man and woman is similar to that in Hemingway's "Hills Like White Elephants": whereas the man takes a "reasonable tone" and is proud to deal with actualities, the woman hypothesizes and asks "what if?" When he finally says he would not have married her if she had been black, the split between them is made emphatic. In the last paragraph the wife moves across the room in total darkness, and his heart pounds as it did on their first night together or when he hears a strange noise in the night—"the sound of someone moving through the house, a stranger." What the story is about is not merely a minor conflict in the life of a particular couple but, rather, the realization of the ultimate strangeness of others, no matter how confident we are that we "know" them. What the story suggests is that strangeness or difference is not skin-deep but profound.

Although marital strife is perhaps the most common subject in modern American short fiction, Ann Beattie probes beyond the ordinary level of this theme by projecting the seemingly inevitable conflicts between married partners outward, onto a metaphoric object or a mirror-image third party. Beattie is not interested in something so ordinary and blatant as adultery as the cause of separation; rather, she focuses on the elusive emotions and subtle tensions that often underlie breakups. Because of their delicate nature, the conflicts Beattie is concerned with cannot be expressed directly and discursively, but instead must be embodied in a seemingly trivial object or an apparently irrelevant other person. One result of this realistic-minimalist technique is that while a story may begin with seemingly pedestrian details, as the details accumulate they begin to take on a lyrical tone and to assume a metaphoric importance.

"Janus," a typical Beattie story about an object, a bowl, that has emotional significance, does not seem to really become a story until the end—when we learn what that emotional significance really is.[11] At the beginning, the bowl seems to be a practical object, something that will help the protagonist, a real estate agent, to sell houses by giving the houses an air of elegance. Gradually, though, we begin to realize that it holds more significance than just that, for the protagonist is obsessed with the object. Moreover, as we read, we may begin to wonder about the significance of the title, for, knowing that Janus is the god of two faces, we are alerted to watch for examples of opposing forces in the story. Perhaps the most basic way in which the bowl is two-faced is generic, in the way that any symbolic or significant object is two-faced; it is both practical and spiritual at the same time, merely an object yet also a meaningful object.

Mary Robison has also often been placed with contemporary "minimalist" writers such as Ann Beattie, Raymond Carver, and Tobias Wolff; like their early modern post-Chekhovian precursors, Mansfield, Anderson, and Joyce, they focus on concrete events and objects in a potentially meaningful situation rather than on a linear narrative. Such stories as "Yours" challenge our usual assumption of what constitutes story.[12] As in Beattie's story "Janus" and Porter's "Theft," the two elements that suggest "storyness" are an oblique background exposition and the transformation of a simple object into something that resonates with meaning. The central objects that hold the story together and give it its poetic resonance and meaning are pumpkins—Alison's four, which look like ordinary children's jack-o'-lanterns, and Clark's four, which look artful and express ferocity, surprise, and serenity. As Clark calls for an emergency unit to come for his wife, who is rapidly losing her battle with cancer, he watches the jack-o'-lanterns. More important, though, they watch him: it is this row of grotesque faces that mock him and his "little talent."

Gabriel García Márquez, Leslie Marmon Silko, Toni Cade Bambara, Cynthia Ozick

The multiculturalism movement of the 1980s has not only broadened the short story canon, it has also introduced new experiments in combining the realism of Chekhov and Joyce with the mythic and linguistic particularities of Latin, Native American, and African American cultures. The best-known example of this combination is the South American writer Gabriel García Márquez, whose "magical realist" style presents events that seem to be given a context of earthly realism but in fact take place in the realm of magic. Like Franz Kafka, who he imitated in his early works, García Márquez creates a world in which human dreams, desires, and fears are objectified as if they existed in the real world. This can be most clearly seen in one of his best-known stories, "A Very Old Man with Enormous Wings."[13] On the one hand, it is hard to take seriously an angel who has wings like a buzzard and who lives in a dung pile; on the other hand, though, there is no way to ignore the fact that he does have wings and therefore objectifies a basic human need for transcendence. Indeed, the story moves from initial scorn of the old man wallowing in the mud to final awe as he flies away across the sea. Because the old man seems too human to be an angel but too angelic to be human the reader is caught between two conflicting emotions.

The reason that the villagers come to prefer the freak with the body of a spider and the head of a maiden over the angel is that where her situation has both a human cause (she disobeyed her parents) and a human moral, the angel's existence seems to have no justification; he is merely, and nothing more than, the mysterious manifestation of the human need for transcendence. Because familiarity breeds contempt, the villagers have normalized him, integrated him into their own ordinary reality. His final transformation into an imaginary dot on the horizon of the sea marks his return to the realm of the transcendent from whence he came.

Leslie Marmon Silko's "Yellow Woman" is, in some ways, the epitome of her work, for, although it takes place in the modern world of jeeps and Jell-O, it also resonates with the primitive world of folktale and legend.[14] What Silko succeeds in doing in this story is yoking a modern woman's fantasy with ancient myth. Since myth is the objectification of desire, the events of "Yellow Woman" seem mythically appropriate, for the story is the embodiment of a reputedly female desire to be carried off by a dark stranger who, although gentle and kind, releases the woman from any possible guilt by a strength of will that compels her to do that which in her fantasy she wishes to do anyway. By identifying the woman with the mythic creature Yellow Woman, the mysterious stranger, transforms her into a goddess who represents the power of all women—huntress, moon goddess, mother of the game, and wife of war. The woman in the story tries to argue with Silva that what they tell in stories was real only back in "time immemorial," but he insists, by his very presence and his claim that he is a katsina, a visitor from the spirit world, and she is Yellow Woman, that the power of the old stories continues.

Although the woman tries to maintain that she has her own time and that she comes from the pueblo on the other side of the mesa, she has been captured by the mythic and truly has no other identity than that of the archetypal Yellow Woman. Her protests that she is not Yellow Woman, that she lives now where there are highways and pickup trucks become weaker and weaker, until finally she is willing to accept her transformation into a creature of legend. She imagines that there will be a story about the day she disappeared when Silva came for her and she did not decide to go, but just went. It is only the intrusion of the reality of the white man who attempts to capture Silva for his rustling that disrupts the fantasy and sends her back home to her husband and children.

Toni Cade Bambara, who calls herself a "Pan-Africanist social-ist feminist," says that writing is one of the ways she participates in struggle. Bambara acknowledges that using the short story as a way to arouse and persuade involves a different technique than does using nonfiction argument. She says that her prefer-ence as a writer and a teacher is indeed the short story, for it "makes a modest appeal for attention, slips up on your blind side and wrassles you to the mat before you know what's grabbed you." Furthermore, she says about her own use of fiction as a method of persuading, "Writing in a rage can produce some interesting pyrotechnics, but there are other ways to keep a fire ablaze, it seems to me. . . . There are hipper ways to get to gut and brain than with hot pokers and pincers."[15]

One of her best-known stories, "The Lesson," communicates its lesson without being didactic.[16] The focus of Bambara's story, although it is based on the social issue of the disparity between the economic status of African Americans and white Americans, is not the social issue itself but one young girl's confrontation with it.

This story is similar to Updike's "A&P" in that the reader's involvement depends on his or her reaction to the young narra-tor. As in "A&P," the language of the narrator is particularly important. On the one hand, the reader may be sympathetic to the speaker because her "hip" language suggests she is confident and self-assured about who she is; on the other hand, the reader may not feel so sympathetic because she is so cocky and resistant to learning anything. Related to the reader's mix of emotions is the fact that the protagonist's feelings about the experience at the FAO Schwartz store is also mixed. On the one hand, there is the sense of the hallowed nature of the store as she compares her experience there to an experience in a Catholic church; on the other hand, there is the sense of the utter obscenity of toys that cost enough to feed a poor family. Finally, there is the ambigu-ous attitude the narrator has toward Miss Moore, who has taken it upon herself to raise the social consciousness of her children. On the one hand, she resents her for her superior ways; on the other hand, she begrudgingly accepts the validity of the "lesson" she is trying to teach. All in all, the story creates a more complex narrative-moral experience for the reader than its obvious social lesson and its clever use of language at first suggests.

Cynthia Ozick is a Jewish short story writer in the tradition of Bernard Malamud: typically, her stories, almost magically blending lyricism and realism, create worlds that are both mythically distant and socially immediate. Although she is also a skilled novelist and poet, as well as the author of a number of essays on Judaism, art, and feminism, it is her short stories that most powerfully reflect her mythic imagination and her poetic use of language. Ozick's most powerful story, "The Shawl," which won first prize in 1981 in the *O. Henry Prize Stories* competition, is about a young Jewish woman in a German concentration camp whose infant is thrown into an electrical fence.[17] It is not solely the event that creates the story's powerful impact, however, as horrible as that event is; it is also the hallucinatory style with which the fiction is created.

The magic of the story is largely due to its viewpoint, which, although it remains with Rosa the mother and reflects her feelings, also exhibits the detached poetry of the nameless narrator. For example, Rosa's dried-up breast, from which the infant Magda cannot suckle, is described as a "dead volcano, blind eye, chill hole"; the infant's budding tooth is cast as "an elfin tombstone of white marble." The perspective of this grotesque poetry reflects the extremity of horror of the Holocaust itself. When we see the knees of Stella (Rosa's teenage niece) as "tumors on sticks," we see the Holocaust as though no ordinary imagery is adequate to capture it, no ordinary voice capable of describing it.

The shawl, which provides a womblike protection for the infant, is magical; buried within it, the child is mistaken for Rosa's breasts. Moreover, when Rosa's milk dries up, the magical shawl nourishes the infant for three days and three nights; as the child sucks on its corner, it provides the "milk of linen." The shawl also is the central object of the story's horrifying climax: when Rosa sees Magda crawling across the central yard of the camp without her comforting shawl and hears her cry out the first sound she has made since the drying up of Rosa's milk, the terrified mother is faced with a crucial decision—to run for the child, even though she knows that her crying will continue without the shawl, or to run for the shawl and take the risk of the child being found first.

When she goes for the shawl, which Stella has taken from the child to wrap around her own thin bones, the scene that follows is straight out of a nightmare—Rosa running with the shawl held high like a talisman, the infant being borne away from the mother over the head of a Nazi guard toward the fence, which hums with its electrical voices. As Magda goes swimming through the air, she looks like a butterfly: "And the moment Magda's feathered round head and her pencil legs and balloonish belly and zigzag arms splashed against the fence, the steel voices went mad in their growling. . . ." Rosa can do nothing, for whatever she does will mean her own death, so she stuffs the shawl into her mouth and "drank Magda's shawl until it dried."

"The Shawl" leaves the reader stunned and breathless with horror. Like the infant Magda herself, the story is practically mute, explaining nothing, simply presenting the event in its magical and mysterious horror. Ozick's follow-up story, "Rosa," is longer, more discursive, more explanatory, more rooted in ordinary reality. It focuses on a few days in the life of Rosa, now a middle-aged woman who lives in a run-down hotel in Miami Beach. The most powerful parts of the story are the letters that Rose writes to her imaginary daughter Magda, in which she invents fictions to retrieve her past. Writing allows her to unlock her tongue, to immerse herself in language and thus to "make a history, to tell, to explain. To retrieve, to retrieve! To lie." In this way, Ozick makes Rosa the image of the writer as parable-maker, telling fictions that have more truth than history does because they are specific, concrete, and laden with emotion and desire rather than mere facts or general and abstract ideas.

Carver's Tribute to Chekhov

Given the importance of Anton Chekhov to the development of the modern short story, it seems appropriate to end this chapter with a brief discussion of the story "Errand," Raymond Carver's poignant farewell tribute to the short story writer's craft and art.[18] Much of the story seems less a unified narrative than a straightforward report of Chekhov's death in a hotel in the resort city of Badenweiler, Switzerland. Without comment, the narrative recounts Chekhov's last hours as a doctor visits him in his room, and his wife Olga Knipper stands by helplessly. Knowing that it is hopeless, and that it is only a matter of minutes, the doctor orders champagne and three glasses from the kitchen. A few minutes after taking a drink, Chekhov dies.

Up to this point, "Errand" is not really a story at all, for it does not have the implied "point" that is typical of the short story—especially since the innovations of Chekhov himself. What makes it a story is the appearance of the young waiter who brings the champagne. When the young man returns to the room the next morning to bring a vase of roses and to pick up the bottle and glasses, Olga Knipper, who has spent the remainder of the night sitting alone with Chekhov's body, urges him to go into the town and find a mortician, someone who takes great pains in his work and whose manner is appropriately reserved.

The young man listens as Olga tells him in great detail what to do. He should, she says, behave as if he is engaged on a great errand, moving down the sidewalk as if he were carrying in his arms a porcelain vase of roses that he must deliver to an important man; he should, she says, raise the brass knocker on the mortician's door and let it fall three times. The mortician will be a modest, unassuming man with a faint smell of formaldehyde on his clothes; as the young man speaks to him, the mortician will take the vase of roses. As Olga tells this "story" of the errand that the young waiter must fulfill, it becomes so real that it seems to be actually happening—in itself an example of the storyteller's art. Meanwhile, the boy is thinking of something else; on the previous night, just after Chekhov died, the cork which the doctor had pushed back into the champagne bottle popped out again and now lies just at the toe of the waiter's shoe. He wants to bend over and pick it up, but does not want to intrude by calling attention to himself. When Olga finishes her storylike description of the errand she wishes him to perform, he leans over, still holding the vase of roses, and without looking reaches down and closes the cork into his hand.

It is this single, simple detail that makes "Errand" a story rather than a mere report and thus a fitting tribute to the art of the short story, both of Chekhov and of Carver. The cork is not a symbol of anything; it is a concrete object in the world that one can almost tangibly feel as the boy closes his hand around it. It is the unique and concrete act of picking up the cork that humanizes the otherwise abstract report of Chekhov's death and makes it into a "story." It embodies the most important lesson that Carver learned from Chekhov—that human meaning is communicated by the simplest of gestures and the most seemingly trivial of objects.

Chapter 6

BIBLIOGRAPHIC ESSAY

Since the 1960s, American literary criticism has gradually shifted from the formalist focus on the individual artwork to what Aristotle termed "the art of literature" in general and its various generic kinds in particular. Especially energetic have been the efforts to establish a poetics for that species of literary art that seems most resistant to theory—narrative prose fiction. However, on making even the most casual survey of these studies, one soon discovers an assumption so pervasive that it is seldom announced, much less questioned: when critics use the terms "prose fiction" or "narrative," primarily they mean the novel.

This attitude that the short story is hardly worth mentioning in the rarefied atmosphere of current "serious" criticism about "serious" literature is not new in Anglo-American literary studies; it is, in fact, as old as criticism of the short story itself. In 1901, in the first full-length study of the form, Brander Matthews noted the "strange neglect" of the short story in literary histories, but for all his efforts to justify the suggestive comments Poe made about the form sixty years earlier, Matthews only succeeded in solidifying critical reaction against the genre.[1] Instead of Matthews's opinion—that the short story is an unique art form differing from the novel in substantive ways—it is the opinion of an anonymous reviewer in the London *Academy* that has remained: "The short story is a smaller, simpler, easier, and less important form of the novel."[2]

One of the many paradoxes of the short story is that from its nineteenth-century historical beginnings it has been the most generically defined of all literary forms, yet it has at the same time been the most neglected by serious theoretical critics. From its genetic birth with Poe's 1842 *Twice-Told Tales* review to Brander Matthews's "philosophy of the short story" at the turn of the century and the many handbooks on the form in the 1920s, the short story has been defined, delineated, and described many times. With the exception of scattered comments by Henry James, William Dean Howells, Joseph Conrad, Stephen Crane, and a few others, however, much of what has been said has been either simplified "how-to" descriptions by popular critics or vague metaphors by admiring practitioners.

Poe's Theories

Because a genre only truly comes into being when the conventions that constitute it are articulated within the larger conceptual context of literature as a whole, Poe's critical comments on the form in the 1830s are largely responsible for the birth of the short story as a unique genre. Poe's notions about the form were not original with him, of course; rather, they derived from the practice and criticism of the German *novelle* in the early part of the century by Goethe, A. W. Schlegel, Ludwig Tieck, and E. T. A. Hoffmann.

Poe first refers to Schlegel's notion of the importance of "totality of interest" in an 1836 review where he argues that although in long works one may be pleased with particular passages, in short pieces, the pleasure results from the perception of the oneness, uniqueness, and overall unity of the work that constitutes a totality of interest or effect.[3] Poe uses the word "plot" in an 1841 review as synonymous with what he means by "unity"; however, he is careful here to distinguish between the usual notion of plot as merely those events which occur one after another and his own definition of plot as an overall pattern, design, or unity.[4]

In his 1842 Hawthorne review, Poe further claims that unity is achieved only in a work that the reader can hold in the mind all at once. After the poem, traditionally the highest of high literary art, Poe says that the short tale has the most potential for being unified. The effect of the tale is synonymous with its overall pattern or plot, which is also synonymous with its theme or idea.[5] Poe carries his concern with unity even further in "The Philosophy of Composition," where he asserts the importance of beginning with the end or effect of the work. Since a narrative cannot be told until the events that it takes as its subject matter have already occurred, the "end" of the events, both in terms of their actual termination and in terms of the purpose to which the narrator binds them, is the "beginning" of the discourse.[6]

The Early Formula Story

Poe's theories about the uniqueness of the short story became firmly embedded within American literary criticism with the publication of Matthews's *The Philosophy of the Short-Story* in 1901, whose title indicates that he was influenced by Poe's "The Philosophy of Composition" as by his *Twice-Told Tales* reviews. Calling the form "Short-story" instead of merely "short story," Matthews argued for the uniqueness of the form by narrowing Poe's "single effect" to mean "a single character, a single event, a single emotion, or the series of emotions called forth by a single situation" (Matthews, 16).

Even then, Matthews's formal rules for the genre might not have had such a disastrous effect if O. Henry had not had such great popular success with his made-to-order formula stories at about the same time. Writers rushed to imitate O. Henry and critics rushed to imitate Matthews. Everyone, they said, could write short stories if they only knew the rules. J. Berg Esenwein's *Writing the Short Story* (1909), Carl H. Grabo's *The Art of the Short Story* (1913), and Blanche Colton Williams's *A Handbook on Story Writing* (1917) are only three of the numerous "how-to" books published in the first twenty years of the century.[7]

Finally, serious readers and critics called for an end to it, filling the quality periodicals with articles on the "decline," "decay," and "senility" of the short story. Gilbert Seldes summed up the reaction at its most extreme in *The Dial* in 1922: "The American short story is by all odds the weakest, most trivial, most stupid, most insignificant art wcrk produced in this country and perhaps in any country."[8] Even Edward J. O'Brien, the greatest champion of the form America has ever had, wrote *The Dance of the Machines* in 1929, censuring the mechanized structure of American society and the machinelike short story that both sprang from it and reflected it.[9]

Because there was so much trading in the short story's marketplace in the first eighty years of its development; because, by the turn of the century, the short story—like that other relatively new American medium, film—had still not disengaged itself from its popular origins and established itself as an art form; because the form had no real tradition or guidance, being a halfbreed offspring of both eighteenth-century restraint and nineteenth-century imagination; for all these reasons it is all the more unfortunate that Brander Matthews's early attempt to give it respectable literary guidance focused too much on restraint and too little on imagination.

However, Matthews did make some suggestions about the form that have since been echoed by other writers and critics. He argued, for example, that the short story has always been popular in America because Americans are more concerned with things unseen than are the English. He was also first to notice that although in the stories of Poe things are realistically or objectively portrayed, a shadow of mystery broods over them. Most critics now recognize that in his psychological first-person narratives, Poe's forcing of psychic responses to such extremes that they seem almost supernatural marks one of his major contributions to the development of the short story as a romantic form.

William Dean Howells in his *Criticism and Fiction* in 1891 claimed that Americans are the finest practitioners of the short story—although, just as typical of his own pragmatic viewpoint, he had a different explanation for the popularity of the form:

It might be argued from the national hurry and impatience that it was a literary form peculiarly adapted to the American temperament, but I suspect that its extraordinary development among us is owing much more to more tangible facts. The success of American magazines, which is nothing less than prodigious, is only commensurate with their excellence.

In 1924, Katherine Fullerton Gerould said that American short story writers have dealt with peculiar atmospheres and special moods because America has no centralized civilization. "The short story does not need a complex and traditional background so badly as the novel does."[10] Ruth Suckow suggested in 1927 that the chaos and unevenness of American life had made the short story a natural expression: life in America was so multitudinous "that its meaning could be caught only in fragments, perceived only by will-of-the-wisp gleams, preserved only in tiny pieces of perfection." Because of the wide divergence of place in America, Americans feel more the multifariousness of life than the English, Suckow argued.[11]

The Short Story's Failed Promise

Soon after Matthews's study of the short story, the first histories of the form appeared, as did a few additional critical-scholarly studies. H. S. Canby's *The Short Story in English* (1909) is a helpful genetic analysis of the form that traces the development of short prose narrative from the *Decameron* and the *Canterbury Tales* up through O. Henry.[12] And Barry Pain's small 1916 pamphlet contains comments on the short story's essentially romantic nature that are still useful. Pain recognized that if Brander Matthews was the first to note the difference between the short story and the novel, his distinctions were so vague that he should not be the last. "If short stories were important enough," Pain challenged, "and it seems to be admitted that they are not—here would be a chance for some very subtle and delicate work on the part of a critic."[13]

With a few exceptions, that "subtle and delicate work" has not been forthcoming. Indeed, a number of critics have made great claims for the future of the short story, only to withdraw their remarks later. William O'Brien concluded his *Advance of the Short Story* by calling short story writers the "destined interpreters of our time to itself and our children."[14] His disillusionment came only six years later with his book *The Dance of the Machines* in which he blasted the mechanical formulas that had taken over short story writing. H. E. Bates ended his 1941 study of the short story by predicting that new writers would find the form essential in the aftermath of "distrustful dislocation" of World War II.[15] More recently, in a new edition of that book, Bates has puzzled about why he was wrong. In 1952, Ray B. West concluded his history of the American short story with a similar unjustified prediction: although complete maturity of the form may or may not have been achieved by the writers of the 1940s, West says, "it seems likely now that we may someday come to view the short story as the particular form through which American letters finally came of age, through which the life of its people and the vision of its artists most nearly approached full expression."[16]

West's prediction has no more been fulfilled than those of O'Brien and Bates. In a four-part symposium on the short story in the *Kenyon Review* in 1968, 1969, and 1970, thirty writers from all over the world sent in their views on the artistic nature of the short story and its current economic status. Almost unanimously they praised the short story as the most natural, yet most artistically demanding, fictional form. However, nearly all lamented that they could not survive by writing short stories and puzzled over why critics ignored the form. The mystery is best summed up by George Garrett:

> Strange that so many of our best writers going way back, have been artists of the short story. Strange that so many of the best young writers coming along, in schools and out, do their best work in the short story form. Strange that the short story has not managed to capture and keep its rightful place.[17]

Although until recently there has been no significant effort to develop a unified approach to the short story, a number of suggestive comments have been made about the short story form since Matthews's book at the turn of the century. However, because the form has been so overshadowed by critical attention to the novel, these remarks were largely ignored until the publication of *Short Story Theories* in 1967, which collected a number of essays on the form and provided an annotated bibliography of many more.[18] Moreover, the form has been so seemingly diverse in subject and structure, and short story criticism has been so pervaded by apparently irreconcilable contradictions, that attempts to define the form have been scoffed at or stymied. For example, in 1927, Ruth Suckow vehemently proclaimed that any attempt to define the short story was a "fundamental stupidity" (Suckow, 317–18); over fifty years later, after surveying the material reprinted in and referred to in *Short Story Theories*, Suzanne Ferguson declared that no single characteristic or cluster of characteristics could be agreed upon by critics that distinguished the short story from other fictions.[19]

And indeed a cursory look at this body of criticism reveals a genre riddled with contradictions. The short story has been called the oldest form of verbal expression, as well as the most recent; it has been called the most natural form of verbal expression, as well as the most conventional and artificial; it has been called the literary form that most adequately reflects human reality as it is actually experienced, as well as the form that reflects only an arbitrary view of human reality. However, these seeming contradictions may be more apparent than real, which is to say, they may result from a failure of critics to make necessary historical distinctions.

Characteristics of the Short Story After Poe

Early histories of the American short story, such as those by H. S. Canby, Fred Lewis Pattee, Alfred C. Ward, and Edward J. O'Brien all attempt to delineate what constitutes the "newness" of the short story after Poe. In his 1909 *The Short Story in English*, Canby argued that the difference between the nineteenth-century short story and previous short narratives is simply the difference between short forms not sharply delineated from other forms and the short story, which is sharply delineated. It is not a difference of kind, he argues, but of degree: the nineteenth-century form shows a higher measure of unity than the older forms. Moreover, the conscious purpose of the short story, argues Canby, a purpose that throws so much emphasis on the climax of a story, is "a vivid realization for the reader of that which moved the author to write, be it incident, be it emotion, be it situation. As a result, he concludes, "the art of the short story becomes as much an art of tone as of incident" (Canby, 303).

In a 1902 study of the short story, Bliss Perry also argued for the importance of tone in the nineteenth-century form, noting that the difference between the older stories (of Boccaccio and Chaucer) and the contemporary story lies not in the originality and ingenuity that Brander Matthews attributed to the form (for the older stories have this also), but rather in the "attitude of the contemporary short story writer toward his material" and in his conscious effort to achieve a certain effect.[20] Although Perry does not specify what this change in attitude is or what kind of effect the short story writer strives for, the stories of Irving, Hawthorne, and Poe suggest that this new attitude of the teller toward his materials results from the romantic awareness that spiritual transcendence is no longer an absolute but, rather, a function of perspective and therefore point of view.

Alfred C. Ward, in his 1924 study of the modern American and English short story, may be right in noting that what links Hawthorne's stories with writers of the twentieth century is that they both "meet in the region of half-lights, where there is commerce between this world and `the other-world.'" However, the difference between short story writers before Hawthorne and those after him is that while this region of half-lights for the pre-romantic writers exists in the external world of myth and the religious externals of allegory, for writers after the romantic shift the realm exists within what James has termed Hawthorne's "deeper psychology."[21]

Many comments about the short story focus on the form's midway relationship between the novel and the lyric poem. Poe himself, of course placed the short story next to the lyric as offering the opportunity for the highest practice of literary art. Most critics since then have not really disagreed, often suggesting the form is closer to the lyric than to its narrative neighbor, the novel. Indeed, except for the fact that the short story shares with the novel the medium of prose, most critics agree that there is a fundamental difference between these two forms. Although the short story is committed to a prose fictional presentation of an event, it makes use of the plurasignification of poetry—a metaphorically overdetermined language, which results either from the basically subjective nature of the form or from its "much-in-little" necessity to use the most suggestive but economical means possible.

By the 1950s, critics were increasingly noting the lyrical nature of the short story and its effort to escape formula plots. Walton Patrick argued that the poetic style appears more consistently in the short story than in the novel because metaphorical dilations are essential to the writer who "strives to pack the utmost meaning into his restricted space."[22] However, predictably, opinion about this effect of this lyricism on the form was split. On the one hand, Herschel Brickell claimed in 1951 that the increase in good short stories, particularly those that were psychological and lyrical, was due to the new surge of creative writing classes in colleges and universities.[23] Falcon O. Baker, in 1953, however, argued that the new crop of college-associated writers, influenced by the New Criticism, had created a new formula to replace the old one, and claimed that the short story was too narrowly the province of the professors and the literary quarterlies.[24]

Implications of the Form's Shortness

While these arguments about the nature of the form went on in such popular magazines as the *Atlantic Monthly* and the *Saturday Review*, literary quarterlies and scholarly journals had little or nothing to say about the form: the effect of the New Criticism on university literature professors was to focus attention on the explication of individual short stories rather than on the generic characteristics of the form itself. Because of a more theoretical approach to the study of literature originated by Russian formalism in the 1920s, European critics have often taken the short story more seriously than the Americans. Russian formalist critic B. M. Éjxenbaum argues in his discussion of O. Henry and the theory of the short story that the novel and the short story are not merely different in kind but are "inherently at odds." The difference between the two forms, says Éjxenbaum, is one of essence, "a difference in principle conditioned by the fundamental distinction between big and small forms."[25]

According to Éjxenbaum, the important implications arising from difference in size centers primarily on the difference between the endings of novels and short stories. Because the novel is structured by the linking of disparate materials and the paralleling of intrigues, the ending usually involves a "point of let-up." The short story, on the other hand, constructed on the basis of a contradiction or incongruity, "amasses its whole weight toward the ending." This built-in necessity of the form has, of course, been the source of much of the popular appeal of the short story but has brought about a great deal of scorn from literary critics. Clearly, not every short story depends on the kind of trick ending for which O. Henry was famous, but there is no way to deny that the shortness of the form seems inevitably to require some sense of intensity or intensification of structure and emphasis on the end—a requirement that is absent in the novel.

Another suggestion about the implications of the shortness of the form has been made by George Lukács in his pre-Marxist *Theory of the Novel* (1920). Perceiving the short story as a fictional form that deals with a "fragment of life," lifted out of life's totality, Lukács says the implication of this delimitation is that the form is stamped with its origin in the author's "will and knowledge." The form is inevitably lyrical because of the author's "form-giving, structuring, delimiting act": its lyricism lies in "pure selection." Yet, for all this lyricism, the short story must deal with event, and the kind of event on which it focuses, says Lukács, is one that "pin-points the strangeness and ambiguity of life," which is to say, one that suggests the arbitrary nature of experiences whose workings are always without cause or reason. The result of the form's focus on "absurdity in all its undisguised and unadorned nakedness" is that the lyricism is concealed behind the "hard outlines of the event" and thus the view of absurdity is given the "consecration of form."[26]

Lukács's discussion of the short story's focus on the absurdity of life is similar to Frank O'Connor's well-known thesis in *The Lonely Voice*—that the short story deals with human loneliness.[27] Perhaps because O'Connor's ideas are intuitive and unsupported by a logically consistent theoretical system, or because his comments are primarily thematic, few critics have felt it worthwhile to follow up O'Connor's ideas. Bernard Bergonzi, however, in his *The Situation of the Novel* (1970) does push O'Connor's notion about loneliness in the form a step further by suggesting that the short story writer is "bound to see the world in a certain way, not merely because of our customary atmosphere of crisis, but because the form of the short story tends to filter down experience to the prime elements of defeat and alienation."[28] The problem of whether the form forces the writer into seeing the world from this particular point of view, or whether the writer with this particular point of view naturally chooses the short story to express it, is not so important as the fact that the short story's shortness has traditionally been closely related to a sense of loneliness and alienation.

This sense of alienation is related to the problematic nature of character in the form. Bliss Perry, in an unusual departure from histories of prose fiction at the turn of the century, devoted a chapter to the short story in his 1902 *A Study of Prose Fiction*. He notes that the shortness of the form requires that character must be "unique, original enough to catch the eye at once"; a result of this need to choose exceptional rather than normal characters is that the short story is "thrown upon the side of romanticism rather than of realism" (Perry, 310).

Many short story writers have agreed that the short story focuses on the exceptional rather than the norm. Henry James once said he rejoiced in the anecdote as a form, defining it as a genre in which something "oddly happened" to someone. And Flannery O'Connor claimed that the form is one in which the writer makes "alive some experience which we are not accustomed to observe everyday, or which the ordinary man may never experience in his ordinary life. . . . Their fictional qualities lean away from typical social patterns, toward mystery and the unexpected."[29] Of her own work she says, it takes its character from "a reasonable use of the unreasonable"—a quality, surely, that both Poe and Hawthorne would have concurred with. "The peculiar problem of the short-story writer," O'Connor says, is how to make action "reveal as much of the mystery of existence as possible . . . how to make the concrete work double time for him."[30]

Given this focus on the unusual and the mysterious, short story writers are forced to control their materials very tightly. As Edith Wharton has said, "the greater the improbability [that is, the further the situation seems to be from real life], the more studied must be the approach. . . . The least touch of irrelevance, the least chill of inattention, will instantly undo the spell."[31] In

1916, Barry Pain suggested that the length of the form creates in the short story something very rarely found in the novel "in the same degree of intensity—a very curious, haunting, and suggestive quality" (Pain, 33).

Few critical studies have been written about the dreamlike, basically romantic nature of the short story. The only extended discussion of this element in the form is Mary Rohrberger's study, which argues that the form embodies a romantic notion of a reality that lies beyond the extensional, everyday world that the novel has always been traditionally concerned with. "The metaphysical view that there is more to the world than that which can be apprehended through the senses provides the rationale for the short story which is a vehicle for the author's probing of the nature of the real. As in the metaphysical view, reality lies beyond the ordinary world of appearances, so in the short story, meaning lies beneath the surface of the narrative."[32]

Sister Mary Joselyn (née Eileen Baldeshwiler) has argued that although all stories have a mimetic base, some stories, which she calls "lyric," have additional elements that we usually associate with verse. Among the poetic elements she notes are "a marked deviation from chronological sequence, the exploitation of purely verbal resources such as tone and imagery, a concentration upon increased awareness rather than upon a completed action, and a high degree of suggestiveness, emotional intensity, achieved with a minimum of means." She goes on to say that the lyric story often has a dual action: a syllogistic plot resting on the onward flow of time and a secondary action expressing "man's attempt to isolate certain happenings from the flux of time, to hold them static, to probe to their inwardness and grasp their meaning. In this respect, the 'lyrical' story bodies forth man's immersion in time and his transcendence of it."[33]

Fifty years separate Fred Lewis Pattee's *The Development of the American Short Story* (1923) and Arthur Voss's *The American Short Story: A Critical Survey* (1973), but their similarities sum up our histories of the form.[34] Both are surveys filled with names, titles, dates, and vague considerations of influence, but neither is critical or theoretical: neither gives us a clear picture of the invariants of the short story that have been sustained throughout the form's history, let alone addresses how one can distinguish these from the variants wrought by historical changes in philosophic perspective, social attitudes, and artistic technique. All our other histories, such as Ray B. West's *Short Story in America: 1900–1950*, Austin Wright's *The American Short Story in the Twenties*, Danforth Ross's *The American Short Story*, and William Peden's *The American Short Story*, are either sketchy, fragmentary, or intentionally narrow in focus.[35]

In 1970, at a seminar held in New York by Doubleday to celebrate the publication of a half century of the O. Henry Award stories, several short story writers, critics, and agents met together to discuss the form. At that time Wallace Stegner reminded us that we do not have—but badly need—a good critical history of the short story, suggesting that the only good criticism of the form is to be found in short story texts.[36] However, a survey of short story texts of the last half century shows that with the exception of Brooks and Warren's *Understanding Fiction*, Gordon and Tate's *House of Fiction*, and Mark Schorer's *Story*, short story texts have not been concerned with critical approaches to the form. Influenced by the New Criticism, short story texts up through the 1950s focused on the "Elements of Fiction," using stories to illustrate the elements of theme, point of view, plot, character, symbol, but making little or no distinction between how these elements function in the short story and in the novel. Swayed by the student cry for "relevance" in the 1960s, short story texts moved even further away from encouraging a systematic study of the form by grouping stories according to thematic categories with even less attention on the form's aesthetic characteristics.

Formal Characteristics of the Short Story

The intensity that manifests itself in the short story does not derive solely from the chosen incident or the manifested theme; rather, it comes from a tight dramatic patterning of the incident in such a way that its dramatic tension is exposed and felt. Danforth Ross, in his study of the American short story, says that Poe's major contribution to short fiction is the way in which he brought tension, long a characteristic of poetry, to the story form. Whereas Irving's stories meander, Poe sought to present a story as a dramatist does in a play.[37] In 1943, Gorham Munson said that "Poe aimed not at a transcription of actuality, but at a patterned dramatization of life." For this, argued Munson, he needed a "storyable incident," an anecdote in the Jamesian sense of something that "oddly happened," an anecdote with a hard nugget of latent value."[38]

This "artificial" patterning of the short story, a heightening of intensity and deepening of significance, has often been a point of controversy among critics. H. S. Canby said in 1901 that whereas the novelist aims at a natural method of transcription, "the author of the short story adopts a very artificial one. His endeavor is to give a striking narrative picture of one phase of the situation or character, disregarding much that a cross section might show." Such a process, says Canby, is very artificial, but also very powerful.[39] A few years later, H. E. Corey condemned this very compression in the short story as pathological: "its unity is abnormally artificial and intense" and leads to titillating our nerves in our pathological moments.[40]

The highly formalistic nature of the short story has also been criticized by those critics and novelists who have affirmed the value of naturalistic presentation and social awareness. Just as the short story was criticized by the naturalist writers in the nineteenth century, it has been scorned by the Marxist writers and critics of the 1930s to the present day. In two essays dating from the 1930s James T. Farrell criticized the form for its sterile formality and its failure to be a vehicle for revolutionary ideology.[41] Maxwell Geismar in 1964 lashed out at the *New Yorker* school of short story writer such as J. D. Salinger, Philip Roth, John Updike, Bernard Malamud, and J. F. Powers for the narrow range of their vision and subject matter, and for the stress they laid on the intricate craftsmanship of the well-made story.[42] Malcolm Cowley has criticized advocates of the so-called antistory as having nothing to write about except their own efforts in finding it difficult to write.[43] More recently, Edward Hyams has said that since art must show man opposed to giant political and industrial institutions, the small, exquisite and intimate art of the short story has nothing to do with our time.[44]

Discussion of the short story by American academic critics, on the other hand, has not been as spirited as the ongoing controversy among the cultural commentators. In fact, professor-critics did not really begin to consider the short story until Cleanth

Brooks and Robert Penn Warren's short story textbook *Understanding Fiction* (1943) made analysis of individual examples of the form respectable by giving the short story equal billing with lyric poetry. A. L. Bader's essay makes the formalist approach to the form quite explicit in 1945: confronting the common complaint that the modern literary short story has no structure, he tries to show that although a narrative structure is still present in the form, its presentation and resolution are so indirect that the reader must work harder to find the perceived relationships of the parts of the story.[45] Walter Sullivan developed this rather simple and general assessment into a more rigid formalist methodology in 1951. Using Mark Schorer's comment that the short story is an art of "moral revelation," Sullivan asserts that the fundamental methodological purpose of the short story is a change from innocence to knowledge—a change that can be either "inter-concatenate" (occurring within the main character) or "extra-concatenate" (occurring within a peripheral character).[46] In 1956, Theodore Stroud, extending Bader and Sullivan's New Critical approaches, focused more on aesthetic than on narrative pattern, arguing that the best way to discern pattern in the short story is to examine how the completeness of a story results from the units or episodes in a work combining to make credible a change in one of the characters or to create a sense of realization in the reader.[47]

General comments about the nature of the short story as a genre were sparse in American criticism during the 1940s and 1950s, not only because the formalist approach of the New Critics focused primarily on individual readings of individual works, but because the Aristotelian approach of the Chicago critics focused primarily on the novel. One notable exception is Norman Friedman's attempt to answer the basic question, "What Makes a Short Story Short?" Taking his approach from Chicago critic Elder Olson's "Outline of Poetic Theory," which itself is taken, in part, from Aristotle's *Poetics*, Friedman argues that a short story is short because the size of the action is short, because the action is static or dynamic, because the author chooses to present in a contracted scale by means of summation and deletion, or because the author chooses a point of view that lends itself to brevity. Although Friedman points out the importance of the length of an action and the manner of presenting it to keep it short, he makes no attempt to deal, as Aristotle did with tragedy, with the kind of action appropriate to the short story form.[48]

Short Story Writers on the Short Story

Whereas serious critical attention to the short story has been sparse and generally unenthusiastic until recently, short story writers have been more faithful advocates of the form, often praising its lyrical and highly aesthetic nature. Most writers have testified to its essentially subjective nature. Sean O'Faolain calls it an "emphatically personal exposition."[49] William Carlos Williams says he thinks it a good medium for "nailing down a single conviction. Emotionally."[50] V. S. Pritchett says the good short story writer knows he is putting on a personal, individual act: he catches "a piece of life as it flies" and makes "his personal performance out of it."[51] Frank O'Connor says that the short story is the nearest fictional form to lyrical poetry: "A novel requires far more logic and far more knowledge of circumstances, whereas a short story can have the sort of detachment from circumstances that lyric poetry has."[52] William Faulkner says that in the novel one can be more careless, put more "trash" in, but "in a short story that's next to the poem, almost every word has to be almost exactly right."[53]

British writer Elizabeth Taylor has suggested that the short story, by its lyrical nature, its sustaining of one mood throughout, can give an impression of "perfection" and the feeling of "being lifted into another world, instead of rather sinking into it, as one does with longer fiction."[54] Maurice Shadbolt says that the challenge of the form is to pull as much of life as the story can bear into the fewest pages and, therefore, to produce, "if possible, that hallucinatory point in which time past and time future seem to co-exist with time present, that hallucinatory point which to me defines the good or great short story."[55] And Torborg Nedreaas of Norway has another metaphor that reveals much about the form: it is like an oval, a drop. "Perhaps because, like a drop, it can absorb and in an instant return a ray of light, the spectrum; or perhaps because it conveys both the transparent and the secretive." Nedreaas says it is often "the atmosphere, the secret glitter, the powerful prose that are the nerve and soul of the short story."[56]

Elizabeth Bowen, in her introduction to the *Faber Book of Modern Short Stories* (1939), made two interesting suggestions about the typical experience the short story deals with and its typical structural difference from the novel, which Frank O'Connor and Nadine Gordimer have since stated more explicitly. Bowen says that the short story, more than the novel, is able to place man alone on that "stage which, inwardly, every man is conscious of occupying alone, and that, exempt as it is from the novel's often forced conclusiveness, the short story may more nearly "approach aesthetic and moral truth."[57] Frank O'Connor develops his well-known thesis about the short story by extending Bowen's first suggestion, claiming that in the short story at its most characteristic we find something we do not find often in the novel—"an intense awareness of human loneliness" (*Lonely Voice*, 19).

Nadine Gordimer's expansion of Bowen's second suggestion perhaps gives us a clue as to why loneliness is so pervasive in the form. Gordimer suggests that the strongest convention of the novel, its prolonged coherence of tone, is false as to the nature of what can be grasped as reality in the modern world. The novel cannot convey that quality of human life "where contact is more like the flash of fireflies, in and out, now here, now there, in darkness." Short story writers, Gordimer says, deal with the only thing one can be sure of—the present moment: "A discrete moment of truth is aimed at—not the moment of truth, because the short story doesn't deal in cumulatives."[58] Perhaps it is not too much to suggest that the relation between O'Connor's theories about the typical short story vision and Gordimer's theories about its typical form are interrelated: the realization of short story characters, that they can depend only on the present moment, is precisely what makes them lonely—and this sense of loneliness is best manifested in a form that focuses only on the present moment.

Eudora Welty, Randall Jarrell, and Joyce Carol Oates have also made suggestive comments about the nature of the short story that are related to the Bowen, O'Connor, and Gordimer ideas. Welty says the most characteristic aspect of the short story is that we cannot see its solid outlines: "it seems bathed in something of its own. It is wrapped in an atmosphere. The first thing we really see about a story is its mystery."[59] Randall Jarrell, in his introduction to *The Anchor Book of Stories*, says that in reading stories we must recall Freud's belief that the "root of all stories is in Grimm, not in La Rochefoucauld; in dreams, not in cameras and tape recorders."[60] And finally Joyce Carol Oates, in a short note in 1971, agrees with Welty that the most interesting thing about the short story is its mystery; but she goes beyond Jarrell to assert that story is the "dream verbalized."[61]

Revival of Critical Interest

Since the late 1970s, literary critics have shown a revival of interest in the short story, some of which may have been sparked by the 1976 publication of *Short Story Theories*, which argued that what was needed was a theory of the form derived from the "underlying vision of the short story, its characteristic mode of understanding and confronting reality." Noted short story critic Susan Lohafer, in a collection of essays on the short story coedited with Jo Ellyn Clarey, *Short Story Theory at a Crossroads*, has called *Short Story Theories* the "first, if not the biggest, move toward a forum for theory."[62] In that same year, in an essay in the journal *Studies in Short Fiction*, I suggested an initial definition of the short story's underlying vision and argued that Poe's description of the form's "unique effect" was consistent with Ernst Cassirer's concept of "mythic perception."[63] In several of my own essays during the 1980s, according to Lohafer, I have become the most consistent proponent of the notion that there is an inherent relationship between a characteristic short story structure and its theme.

It is this very issue—whether a unified generic definition of the short story is possible—that divided short story theorists in the 1980s into two groups. One of the most influential among those who do not believe that such a generic description is possible is Mary Louise Pratt; disagreeing with those who argued that the short story is a primary form, she has claimed that because the novel has always been more prestigious and powerful as a genre, the development of the short story has been secondarily conditioned by the novel. Pratt has rejected the possibility that a generic determination of the characteristics of a genre like the short story will ever be possible.[64]

Books on the short story in the 1980s dealt only unevenly with generic issues. For example, Walter Allen's 1981 survey is a traditional discussion, valuable for the way in which it provides a framework for understanding the development of the form; it does not, however, attempt to formulate a generic approach.[65] Valerie Shaw's desultory discussion of the form in 1983 disparages any attempt at a theoretical approach.[66] Helmut Bonheim's 1982 study of narrative modes of the short story, based on a statistical study of the form—particularly of short story endings—focuses on only a limited set of short story techniques.[67] John Gerlach's 1985 analysis of the concept of closure in the American short story is a helpful study of an important element of the form, but it is somewhat narrowly focused both theoretically and in the number of stories examined.[68] John Bayley's 1988 discussion of typical poetic techniques and devices common to the form from Henry James to Elizabeth Bowen, and Clare Hanson's 1985 study of the authority of the teller in the form between 1880 and 1980 are both suggestive contributions; both, however, focus on quite limited historical periods.[69]

Collections of essays on the short story published during the 1980s include *The Teller and the Tale*, edited by Wendell Aycock, and *Re-Reading the Short Story*, edited by Clare Hanson, both of which include original but not very incisive essays on a number of aspects of the form.[70] The most important collections of theoretical essays on the form in the 1980s are the special issue of *Modern Fiction Studies* published in 1982 and *Short Story Theory at a Crossroads*, edited by Susan Lohafer and Jo Ellen Clarey in 1989. The former is especially notable for two suggestive essays: Suzanne Hunter Brown's discussion of two readings of a section from Thomas Hardy's *Tess of the D'Ubervilles*—as a short story and as part of a novel—which argues that we read identical texts differently depending on what genre frame of expectations we bring to them; and Suzanne Ferguson's argument that the modern short story is not a discrete genre, different from the sketch and tale that went before it, but rather a manifestation of the techniques and assumptions of literary impressionism.[71]

Both Brown and Ferguson have essays in Lohafer and Clarey's *Short Story Theory at a Crossroads*: Ferguson demonstrates how social factors influenced the rise and fall of the prestige of the short story, and Brown provides a helpful analytical survey of research being done by psychologists of discourse on the nature of storyness and cognitive responses to literature. Also included in this volume are essays by critics already mentioned in this survey: Norman Friedman, who reviews and critiques a number of contemporary theorists; Mary Rohrberger, who disagrees with Friedman's strictly scientific approach to a definition of the form; Austin Wright, who argues for a formalist view of genre as a cluster of conventions; and my own essay on the shift from mythic to metaphoric motivation in the early development of the form during the American romantic period.

Twayne Publishers has provided a significant boost to this revival of interest in the short story in the 1980s with two series of books: Critical History of the Short Story and Studies in Short Fiction. While the first series features historical-critical survey essays on English, American, Russian, Irish, and Latin American short fiction, the second focuses on the short fiction of individual authors, including my own attempt to clarify the basic nature of Poe's contribution to the development of the short story as a genre both in his criticism and his own fiction.

By and large, the burgeoning of interest in literary theory since the 1960s has not had a significant effect on criticism of the short story, despite the fact that the genre's quite formal nature would seem to invite formalist, structuralist, and poststructuralist readings. Frederic Jameson, in one of the best early surveys of formalism and structuralism, has suggested that structuralism would find the short story more amenable to its own brand of analysis than it does the novel, for where the novel has no pre-existing laws that govern its form, the short story or tale is "characterized by a specific and determinate kind of content" and thus its laws can be the object of investigation.[72] However, although narratologists such as Roland Barthes and Tzvetan Todorov have focused on short forms, this stems less from their interest in the form than from the fact that their intensive analyses of grammatical structure is too burdensome to sustain over the long haul of the novel.[73] Representative examples of the sometimes tedious thoroughness of the structuralist approach to short fiction that made it die of its own weight are Seymour Chatman's essay "New Ways of Analyzing Narrative Structure," with its detailed analysis of James Joyce's story "Eveline," and Gerald Prince's *A Grammar of Stories*, which attempts to account for the structure of all syntactical sets that readers intuitively recognize as stories.[74]

Cognitive Psychology, Computers, and the Short Story

Perhaps a more fruitful area for the scientific study of short narrative—a hope structuralism was unable to sustain—may lie in the union of short story criticism with studies in cognitive science. Cognitive research has shown, as reader response theorists have previously insisted, that the knowledge of the world that readers bring to a story determines their understanding of it. Most of the recent empirical research on the narrative reading process began in the 1970s with the introduction of such concepts as "frame" by Marvin Minksy, "script" by Robert Abelson and Robert Schank, and "schemata" by David Rumelhart and others. The Dutch journal *Poetics* has been the most instrumental in promoting this kind of study of the short story, devoting a special issue to the form in 1988. The literary critic most active in this new area of research is Susan Lohafer, whose earlier (1983) book *Coming to Terms with the Short Story* was an important full-length theoretical study.[75] In a series of essays since then, Lohafer has been concerned with the reader's understanding of "storyness, particularly what she calls "preclosure"—those points in a story when a reader senses that a story could but does not end.[76]

Because of scientific and commercial interest in artificial intelligence, modern technology has stimulated much of the current research on how the human mind processes information, as well as how computers can simulate those mental processes. Moreover, the computer's ability to provide random rather than linear access to information may also change forever the way that writers write stories and readers read them. Robert Coover is currently experimenting with the creation of fiction in a "hypertext" format, in which multiple and indeterminate links rather than a linear temporal progression structures the story. Using the computer program *Storyspace*, such writers as Michal Joyce, David Bolter, and Stuart Moulthrop have developed hypertexts that attempt to defeat the linearity of printed texts. My own short story textbook *Fiction's Many Worlds* is accompanied by computer disks in which a number of stories are provided in an interactive hypertext format that enables readers to break up their narrative linearity and reorganize them spatially for analytical understanding.[77] My article in the *Technological Horizons in Education*

Journal provides the basis for such an approach to reading short narrative by outlining the relationship between current intertextual literary theory and modern discourse theory.[78] Noted critic Susan Lohafer is currently compiling an anthology of new essays by a number of literary critics and psychologists on cognitive approaches to the short story; the genre's extremely patterned and formal nature may make it an ideal means by which future researchers can discover how humans create and respond to "storyness."

The renewed critical attention to the short story since the late 1960s, combined with the so-called renaissance of interest in the form by contemporary writers in the 1980s, is ample evidence that the short story is enjoying more respect than it ever has before.[79] The large attendance and the enthusiastic response to the Second and Third Annual Conferences of the Society for the Study for the Short Story held at Northern Iowa University, the University of Iowa, and Iowa State University in the summers of 1992 and 1994 is only one such indication. Hundreds of attendees discussed the short story with John Barth, Joyce Carol Oates, Leslie Marmon Silko, Ann Beattie, Tobias Wolff, Bharati Mukherjee, Amy Tan, and many other short story writers and critics. No longer tainted by commercialism as it was in the early years of the century, and heir now to one hundred and fifty years of vigorous artistic experimentation and perceptive critical discussion, the short story may have finally come into its own as a literary genre deserving of serious theoretical consideration.

Notes and References

1. Overview

1. Ernst Cassirer, *Language and Myth*, trans. Susanne K. Langer (New York: Dover Publications, 1947), 33.

2. Philip Wheelwright, *The Burning Fountain* (Bloomington: Indiana University Press, 1968), 148–53.

3. In *The Sacred and the Profane*, trans. Willard R. Trask (New York: Harcourt, Brace, 1959), Eliade says that the sacred "always manifests itself as a reality of a wholly different order from 'natural' realities" (10).

4. B. M. Éjxenbaum, *O. Henry and the Theory of the Short Story*, trans. I. R. Titunik (Ann Arbor: University of Michigan, 1968), 4.

5. Francesco De Sanctis, "Boccaccio and the Human Comedy," trans. Lucio Bartolai, in Boccaccio, *The Decameron*, ed. Mark Musa and Peter E. Bondanella (New York: W. W. Norton, 1977), 217.

6. Ian Watt, *The Rise of the Novel* (Berkeley and Los Angeles: University of California Press, 1967), 32.

7. Charles C. Mish, "English Short Fiction in the Seventeenth Century," *Studies in Short Fiction* 6 (1969): 223–330.

8. Benjamin Boyce, "English Short Fiction in the Eighteenth Century: A Preliminary View," *Studies in Short Fiction* 5 (1968): 96.

9. Edward Pilcher, "On the Conventions of Eighteenth-Century British Short Fiction," *Studies in Short Fiction* 12 (1975): 199–203.

10. Throughout this study I use the term "folktale" to refer to a wide range of short narratives from an oral tradition, including fairy tales, legends, myths, and fables. Such tales often feature characters who are relatively two-dimensional projections (of psychic states, desires, fears, wishes, anxieties, and so on) and are usually highly formal and patterned rather than realistic. When I wish to emphasize individual characteristics of these forms, such as their moral purpose or their emphasis on the realm of "fairy," I shall use more specific terms, such as "fable" and "fairy tale."

11. Robert Langbaum, *The Poetry of Experience* (New York: W. W. Norton, 1957), 42–45.

12. Quoted in *Storytellers and Their Art*, ed. Georgianne Trask and Charles Burkhart (New York: Doubleday Anchor, 1963), 25–26.

13. Fred Lewis Pattee, *The Development of the American Short Story* (New York: Harper and Row, 1923), 3.

14. Edward J. O'Brien, *The Advance of the American Short Story*, rev. ed. (New York: Dodd, Mead, 1931), 22–24.

15. H. S. Canby, *The Short Story in English* (New York: Holt, Rinehart and Winston, 1909, rpt. 1932), 300.

16. Northrop Frye, *Anatomy of Criticism* (Princeton: Princeton University Press, 1957), 304–6.

17. Horace Walpole, "Preface to the Second Edition," *The Castle of Otranto* (New York: Macmillan Publishing, 1973), 19.

18. Alfred C. Ward, *Aspects of the Modern Short Story: English and American* (London: University of London Press, 1924), 16–17.

19. Robert F. Marler, "From Tale to Short Story: The Emergence of a New Genre in the 1850's," *American Literature* 46 (1974): 162.

20. Ray B. West, *The Short Story in America: 1900–1950* (Chicago: Henry Regnery, 1952), 13.

21. Although Hawthorne, and less frequently Poe, also wrote long narratives, both make it quite clear that their primary concern in these longer fictions was to fabricate an aesthetic universe, as the romance writers did, rather than to create the similitude of the external world after the fashion of the novelists.

22. Ambrose Bierce, "The Short Story," *The Collected Works of Ambrose Bierce*, vol. 10 (1911; rpt. New York: Gordian Press, 1966), 243.

23. Henry James, "The Art of Fiction," in *Realism and Romanticism in Fiction*, ed. Eugene Current-García and Walton R. Patrick (Chicago: Scott, Foresman, 1962), 97.

24. Henry James, "On the Genesis of 'The Real Thing,'" in *What is the Short Story?* rev. ed., ed. Eugene Current-García and Walton R. Patrick (Chicago: Scott, Foresman, 1975), 25.

25. *Stephen Crane: Letters*, ed. R. W. Stallman and Lillian Gilkes (New York: New York University Press, 1960), 154.

26. Eugene Current-García, *O. Henry* (New York: Twayne Publishers, 1965), 156.

27. Lionel Stevenson, "The Short Story in Embryo," *English Literature in Transition* 15 (1972): 261–68.

28. Frank O'Connor, *The Lonely Voice: A Study of the Short Story*. (Cleveland: World Publishing, 1963).

29. Wendell Harris, "Vision and Form: The English Novel and the Emergence of the Short Story," *Victorian Newsletter* 47 (1975), 11.

30. Robert Louis Stevenson, "A Humble Remonstrance," in *Realism and Romanticism in Fiction*, ed. Eugene Current-García and Walton R. Patrick (Chicago: Scott, Foresman, 1962), 113–14.

31. Lionel Stevenson, "The Short Story in Embryo," *English Literature in Transition* 15 (1972): 268; Walter Allen, *The Short Story in English* (Oxford: Clarendon Press, 1981), 14.

32. Trilling's essay from *The Liberal Imagination* is reprinted in *Kipling and the Critics*, ed. Elliot L. Gilbert (New York University Press, 1965), 89–98; Wilson's essay from *The Wound and the Bow* is reprinted in *Kipling's Mind and Art*, ed. Andrew Rutherford (Stanford: Stanford University Press, 1964), 17–69.

33. Letter to Edmund Gosse, March 1, 1915. Cited by Charles Burkhart, "The Short Stories of George Moore," in *The Man of Wax*, ed. Douglas Hughes (New York: New York University Press, 1971), 224.

34. Bonaro Overstreet, "Little Story, What Now?" *Saturday Review of Literature* 24 (1941): 4.

35. Austin Wright, *The American Short Story in the Twenties*. (Chicago: University of Chicago Press, 1961), 149–51.

36. Frank O'Connor, *The Lonely Voice: A Study of the Short Story* (Cleveland: World Publishing, 1963), 23.

37. Cowley uses the phrase in his introduction to *The Portable Hemingway* (New York: Viking Press, 1945).

38. Isak Dinesen, "The Cardinal's First Tale," *Last Tales* (New York: Vintage, 1975), 24–26.

2. Nineteenth-Century Beginnings

1. Frank O'Connor, *The Lonely Voice: A Study of the Short Story* (Cleveland: World Publishing, 1963), 15.

2. B. M. Éjxenbaum, "The Structure of Gogol's 'The Overcoat,'" trans. Beth Paul and Muriel Nesbitt, *The Russian Review* 22 (1963): 377–99.

3. Horace Walpole, "Preface to the Second Edition," *The Castle of Otranto*, in *Three Gothic Novels*, ed. Peter Fairclough (New York: Penguin Books, 1968), 43–44.

4. Frank O'Connor, *The Lonely Voice: A Study of the Short Story* (Cleveland: World Publishing, 1963), 19.

5. I discuss this issue in more detail in chapters 3 and 4, particularly in the stories of Chekhov, Hemingway, Mansfield, and Joyce.

6. Erich Fromm, *The Art of Loving* (New York: Harper, 1956), 9.

7. Edgar Allan Poe, "The Fall of the House of Usher," *The Complete Tales and Poems of Edgar Allan Poe* (New York: Random House, 1938), 231; hereafter cited in text as "Usher."

8. Jean Ricardou, "The Story Within the Story," trans. Joseph Kestner, *James Joyce Quarterly* 18 (1981): 323–38.

9. Herman Melville, "Bartleby," in *Herman Melville: Four Short*

Novels (New York: Bantam, 1959), 3; hereafter cited in text as "Bartleby."

10. Roman Jakobson, "Two Aspects of Language: Metaphor and Metonymy," *European Literary Theory*, ed. Vernon W. Gras (New York: Dell, 1973), 124.

11. Elizabeth Hardwick, *Bartleby in Manhattan and Other Essays* (New York: Random House, 1983), 244.

12. Robert Marler, "'Bartleby, the Scrivener'" and the American Short Story," *Genre* 6 (1973): 431.

13. Newton Arvin, *Herman Melville* (New York: Viking, 1950), 242.

14. Robert F. Marler, "From Tale to Short Story: The Emergence of a New Genre in the 1850's," *American Literature* 46 (1974): 162.

15. Erich Heller, "The Realistic Fallacy," *Documents of Modern Literary Realism*, ed. George J. Becker (Princeton: Princeton University Press, 1963), 596.

3. Nineteenth-Century Realism

1. Bret Harte, "The Development of the Short Story," *Cornhill Magazine* 7 (1899); reprinted in *What IS the Short Story?*, ed. Eugene Current-García and Walton Patrick (Glenview, Ill.: Scott, Foresman, rev. ed. 1974), 29.

2. See Susan Lohafer, "Preclosure and Story Processing," in *Short Story Theory at a Crossroads*, ed. Susan Lohafer and Jo Ellyn Clarey (Baton Rouge: Louisiana State University Press, 1989), 249–75.

3. B. M. Éjxenbaum, *O. Henry and the Theory of the Short Story*, trans. I. R. Titunik (Ann Arbor: University of Michigan, 1968), 7.

4. Frederick Karl, *A Reader's Guide to Joseph Conrad* (New York: Farrar, Straus and Giroux, 1969), 231.

5. Joseph Conrad, "The Secret Sharer," *Conrad's Secret Sharer and the Critics*, ed. Bruce Harkness (Belmont, Calif.: Wadsworth, 1962), 4; hereafter cited in text as "Secret Sharer."

6. Albert Guerard, *Conrad the Novelist* (Cambridge, Mass.: Harvard University Press, 1958), 22.

7. Thomas Mann, "Freud and the Future," *Essays of Three Decades*, trans. H. T. Lowe-Porter (New York: Alfred A. Knopf, 1947), 311–23.

8. Robert Langbaum, "The Mysteries of Identity," *The Modern Spirit* (New York: Oxford University Press, 1970), 175–77.

9. Cited in Chekhov: *The Critical Heritage*, ed. Victor Emeljanow (London: Routledge and Kegan Paul, 1981), 70; hereafter cited in text as *Critical Heritage*.

10. Conrad Aiken, "Anton Chekhov," *Collected Criticism* (New York: Oxford University Press, 1968), 151.

11. John Barth, *The Friday Book* (New York: G. P. Putnam's Sons, 1984), 221.

12. Mark Schorer, *The Story*, 2nd ed. (Englewood Cliffs, New Jersey: Prentice Hall, 1967), 57.

13. Anton Chekhov, *Letters on the Short Story, the Drama, and Other Literary Topics*, ed. Louis S. Friedland (New York: Dover, 1966), 64.

14. James Joyce, *Stephen Hero* (London: Jonathan Cape, 1944), 188.

15. David Daiches, "*Dubliners*," *Twentieth Century Interpretations of Dubliners*, ed. Peter K. Garrett (Englewood Cliffs, N.J.: Prentice-Hall, 1968), 32.

16. James Joyce, "The Dead," *Dubliners*, ed. Robert Scholes (New York: Viking, 1969), 213.

17. Although both Joyce's *Dubliners* and Anderson's *Winesburg, Ohio* are significant innovations in the development of the modern short story, both have been referred to as "composite novels." I, however, prefer the designation "short story cycle," for the stories in these books are less integral parts of a novel than intense, self-sufficient stories linked only loosely together. See Forrest L. Ingram, S. J., "The Dynamics of Short Story Cycles," *New Orleans Review* 2 (1979): 7–12.

18. Rex Burbank, *Sherwood Anderson* (Boston: Twayne Publishers, 1964).

19. Sister Mary Joselyn, O.S.B., "Sherwood Anderson and the Lyric Story," in *The Twenties: Poetry and Prose*, ed. Richard E. Langford and William E. Taylor (Deland, Fla.: Everette Edwards, 1966), 70–77.

20. David D. Anderson, *Sherwood Anderson: An Introduction and Interpretation* (New York: Holt, Rinehart, and Winston, 1967).

4. Early-Twentieth-Century Formalism

1. The Chekhov quotation is from *Letters on the Short Story, the Drama, and Other Literary Topics*, ed. Louis S. Friedland. (New York: Dover, 1966); the Hemingway quotation is from *Death in the Afternoon* (New York: Charles Scribner's Sons, 1932).

2. "Hills Like White Elephants," in *The Short Stories of Ernest Hemingway* (New York: Charles Scribner's Sons, 1953), 273–78.

3. Eudora Welty, "The Eye of the Story," *Yale Review* 55 (1966), 265–74.

4. Robert Penn Warren, "Irony with a Center: Katherine Anne Porter," *Selected Essays* (New York: Random House, 1951), 136–56.

5. "Flowering Judas," *The Collected Stories of Katherine Anne Porter* (New York: New American Library, 1969), 90–102.

6. "A Rose for Emily," *The Faulkner Reader* (New York: Random House, 1954), 489–97.

7. "The World of Love: The Fiction of Eudora Welty," in *The Creative Present*, ed. Nona Balakian and Charles Simmons (Garden City, N.Y.: Doubleday, 1963), 182.

8. "Keela, the Outcast Indian Maiden," *Selected Stories of Eudora Welty* (New York: Modern Library, 1943), 74–88.

9. "Introduction," *Selected Stories of Eudora Welty* (New York: Modern Library, 1943), xxi.

10. "The Magic Barrel," *The Magic Barrel* (New York: Dell, 1959), 169–88.

11. Earl Rovit, "The Jewish Literary Tradition," in *Bernard Malamud and the Critics*, ed. Leslie A. Field and Joyce C. Field (New York: New York University Press, 1970), 7.

12. Mark Goldman, "Comic Vision and the Theme of Identity," in *Bernard Malamud and the Critics*, 156.

13. B. M. Éjxenbaum, *O. Henry and the Theory of the Short Story*, trans. I. R. Titunik (Ann Arbor: University of Michigan Slavic Contributions, 1968), 6.

14. *The Stories of Bernard Malamud* (New York: Farrar, Straus and Giroux, 1983), iii.
15. "The Snake," *The Long Valley* (New York: Viking, 1938).
16. "The Swimmer," *The Stories of John Cheever* (New York: Ballantine, 1980), 713–24.

5. Contemporary Renaissance

1. "Philosophy and the Form of Fiction," *Fiction and the Figures of Life* (New York: Knopf, 1970), 24.
2. *The Friday Book* (New York: G. P. Putnam's Sons, 1984).
3. "Autobiography," *Lost in the Funhouse* (New York: Bantam, 1969).
4. "After Joyce," *Location* 2 (Summer 1964): 13–16.
5. "The Balloon," *Sixty Stories* (New York: G. P. Putnam's Sons, 1981).
6. Raymond Carver, "Neighbors," in *Will You Please Be Quiet, Please?* (New York: McGraw-Hill, 1978).
7. Raymond Carver, "Why Don't You Dance?" in *What We Talk About When We Talk About Love* (New York: Knopf, 1981).
8. Raymond Carver, "Cathedral," in *Where I'm Calling From* (New York: Atlantic Monthly Press, 1988).
9. Raymond Carver, "The Bath," in *What We Talk About When We Talk About Love* (New York: Knopf, 1981); "A Small, Good Thing," in Where I'm Calling From (New York: Atlantic Monthly Press, 1988).
10. Tobias Wolff, "Say Yes," in *Back in the World* (New York: Houghton Mifflin, 1985).
11. Ann Beattie, "Janus," in *Where You'll Find Me* (New York: Simon and Schuster, 1986).
12. Mary Robison, "Yours," in *An Amateur's Guide to the Night* (New York: Knopf, 1983).
13. Gabriel García Márquez, "A Very Old Man with Enormous Wings," in *Leaf Storm and Other Stories* (New York: HarperCollins, 1972).
14. Leslie Marmon Silko, "The Yellow Woman," reprinted in *Fiction's Many Worlds*, ed. Charles E. May (Lexington, Mass.: D. C. Heath, 1993).

15. Toni Cade Bambara, "What It Is I Think I'm Doing Anyhow," in *The Writer on Her Work*, ed. Janet Sternburg (New York: Norton, 1980).

16. Toni Cade Bambara, "The Lesson," in *Gorilla, My Love* (New York: Random House, 1972).

17. Cynthia Ozick, *The Shawl* (New York: Knopf, 1989).

18. "Errand," in *Where I'm Calling From* (New York: Atlantic Monthly Press, 1988).

6. Bibliographic Essay

1. Brander Matthews, *The Philosophy of the Short-Story* (New York: Longmans, Green, 1901); hereafter cited in text.

2. Anonymous, "Review of Brander Matthews' *Philosophy of the Short-Story*," Academy (London), March 30, 1901; reprinted in Current-García and Walton R. Patrick, *What Is the Short Story?* (New York: Scott, Foresman, rev. ed. 1974), 48–50.

3. Edgar Allan Poe, *Southern Literary Messenger*, January 1836; reprinted in Charles E. May, *Edgar Allan Poe: A Study of the Short Fiction* (Boston: Twayne Publishers, 1991), 118.

4. Edgar Allan Poe, *Graham's Magazine*, April, 1841; reprinted in May, *Edgar Allan Poe*, 120.

5. Edgar Allan Poe, *Graham's Magazine*, May, 1842; reprinted in May, *Edgar Allan Poe*, 124–26.

6. Edgar Allan Poe, *Graham's Magazine*, April, 1846; reprinted in May, *Edgar Allan Poe*, 127–29.

7. J. Berg Esenwein, *Writing the Short Story: A Practical Handbook on the Rise, Structure, Writing and Sale of the Modern Short Story* (New York: Hinds, Noble and Eldredge, 1909); Carl H. Grabo, *The Art of the Short Story* (New York: Charles Scribner's Sons, 1913); Blanche Colton Williams, *A Handbook on Story Writing* (New York: Dodd, Mead, 1917).

8. Gilbert Seldes, "The Best Butter," *Dial* 72 (1922), 427–30.

9. Edward O'Brien, *The Dance of the Machines: The American Short Story and the Industrial Age* (New York: Macaulay, 1929).

10. Katherine Fullerton Gerould, "The American Short Story," *Yale Review* NS 13 (1924): 642–63.

11. Ruth Suckow, "The Short Story," in *Saturday Review of Literature* 4 (1927): 317–18; hereafter cited in text.

12. H. S. Canby, *The Short Story in English* (New York: Holt, Rinehart and Winston, 1909, rpt. 1932); hereafter cited in text.

13. Barry Pain, *The Short Story* (London: Martin Secker, 1916), 52; hereafter cited in text.

14. Edward J. O'Brien, *The Advance of the American Short Story* (New York: Dodd, Mead, rev. ed. 1931).

15. H. E. Bates, *The Modern Short Story*: A Critical Survey (Boston: The Writer, 1941, rev. ed. 1972).

16. Ray B. West, *The Short Story in America: 1900–1950* (Chicago: Henry Regnery, 1952), 122.

17. George Garrett, "United States," *Kenyon Review* 31:4 (1969), 464.

18. Charles E. May, *Short Story Theories* (Athens: Ohio University Press, 1967).

19. Suzanne C. Ferguson, "Defining the Short Story: Impressionism and Form," *Modern Fiction Studies* 28 (1982): 13; hereafter cited as Ferguson.

20. Bliss Perry, "The Short Story," in *A Study of Prose Fiction*, (Boston and New York: Houghton Mifflin, 1902): 303; hereafter cited in text.

21. Alfred C. Ward, *Aspects of the Modern Short Story: English and American* (London: University of London Press, 1924), 19.

22. Walton Patrick, "Poetic Style in the Contemporary Short Story," *College Composition and Communication* 18 (1957): 77–84.

23. Herschel Brickell, "What Happened to the Short Story?" *Atlantic Monthly* 188 (1951): 74–76.

24. Falcon O. Baker, "Short Stories for the Millions," *Saturday Review* 19 (1953): 7–9, 48–49.

25. B. M. Éjxenbaum, *O. Henry and the Theory of the Short Story*, trans. I. R. Titunik (Ann Arbor: University of Michigan Slavic Contributions, 1968), 4.

26. George Lukács, *The Theory of the Novel*, trans. Anna Bodtock (Cambridge, Mass.: MIT Press, 1971), 51–52.

27. Frank O'Connor, *The Lonely Voice: A Study of the Short Story* (Cleveland: World Publishing, 1963); hereafter cited in text.

28. Bernard Bergonzi, *The Situation of the Novel* (London: Macmillan, 1970), 215–16.

29. Flannery O'Connor, "The Grotesque in Southern Fiction," in *Mystery and Manners*, ed. Sally and Robert Fitzgerald (New York: Farrar, Straus and Giroux, 1969), 40.

30. Flannery O'Connor, "Writing Short Stories," in *Mystery and Manners*, ed. Sally and Robert Fitzgerald (New York: Farrar, Straus and Giroux, 1969), 98.

31. Edith Wharton, "Telling a Short Story," in *The Writing of Fiction* (New York: Charles Scribner's Sons, 1925), 33–58.

32. Mary Rohrberger, *Hawthorne and the Modern Short Story: A Study in Genre* (The Hague: Mouton, 1966), 141.

33. Eileen Baldeshwiler, "The Lyric Short Story: The Sketch of a History," *Studies in Short Fiction* 6 (1969): 443–53.

34. Fred Lewis Pattee, *The Development of the American Short Story* (New York: Harper and Row, 1923); Arthur Voss, *The American Short Story: A Critical History* (Norman: University of Oklahoma Press, 1973).

35. Ray B. West, *Short Story in America: 1900–1950* (Chicago: Henry Regnery, 1952); Austin Wright, *The American Short Story in the Twenties* (Chicago: University of Chicago Press, 1961); Danforth Ross, *The American Short Story* (Minneapolis: University of Minnesota Press, 1961); William Peden, *The American Short Story: Front Line in the National Defense of Literature* (Boston: Houghton Mifflin, 1964); revised and retitled *The American Short Story: Continuity and Change, 1940–1975*, (1975).

36. "Short Stories: Past, Present, and Future," *Publishers Weekly* 198 (Dec. 14, 1970), 12–15.

37. Danforth Ross, *The American Short Story* (Minneapolis: University of Minnesota Press, 1961), 8.

38. Gorham Munson, "The Recapture of the Storyable," *The University Review* 10 (1943): 37–44.

39. H. S. Canby, "On the Short Story," *Dial* 31 (1901): 271–73.

40. Herbert Ellsworth Cory, "The Senility of the Short Story," *Dial* 62 (1917): 379–81.

41. James T. Farrell, "Nonsense and the Short Story," and "The Short Story," in *The League of Frightened Philistines and Other Papers* (New York: Vanguard Press, 1945), 72–81, 136–48.

42. Maxwell Geismar, "The American Short Story Today," *Studies on the Left* 4 (1964): 21–27.

43. Malcolm Cowley, "Storytelling's Tarnished Image," *Saturday Review* 25 (Sept. 1971): 25–27, 54.

44. Edward Hyams, "England," *Kenyon Review* 32 (1970): 89–95.

45. A. L. Bader, "The Structure of the Modern Short Story," *College English* 7 (1945): 86–92.

46. Walter Sullivan, "Revelation in the Short Story: A Note on Methodology," *Vanderbilt Studies in Humanities* vol. 1, ed. Richard C. Beatty, John Philip Hyatt, and Monroe K. Spears (Nashville: Vanderbilt University Press, 1951), 106–12.

47. Theodore A. Stroud, "A Critical Approach to the Short Story," *The Journal of General Education* 9 (1956): 91–100.

48. Norman Friedman, "What Makes a Short Story Short?" *Modern Fiction Studies* 4 (1958): 103–17.

49. Sean O'Faolain, *The Short Story* (New York: Devin-Adair, 1951).

50. William Carlos Williams, *A Beginning on the Short Story: Notes* (Yonkers, N.Y.: Alicat Bookshop Press, 1950).

51. V. S. Pritchett, "Short Stories," *Harper's Bazaar* 87 (July 1953): 31, 113.

52. Frank O'Connor, quoted in *Storytellers and Their Art*, ed. Georgianne Trask and Charles Burkhart (Garden City, N.Y.: Doubleday, 1963), 21.

53. William Faulkner, quoted in *Storytellers and Their Art*, 25.

54. Elizabeth Taylor, "England," *Kenyon Review* 31 (1969): 471.

55. Maurice Shadbolt, "New Zealand," *Kenyon Review* 31 (1969): 70.

56. Torborg Nedreaas, "Norway," *Kenyon Review* 31 (1969): 459.

57. Elizabeth Bowen, "The Faber Book of Modern Short Stories," in *Short Story Theories*, ed. Charles E. May (Athens: Ohio University, 1967), 158.

58. Nadine Gordimer, "The Flash of Fireflies," in *Short Story Theories*, 180.

59. Eudora Welty, "The Reading and Writing of Short Stories," in *Short Story Theories*, 163.

60. Randall Jarrell, "Stories," in *Short Story Theories*, 35.

61. Joyce Carol Oates, "The Short Story," *Southern Humanities Review* 5 (1971): 213–14.

62. *Short Story Theory at a Crossroads*, ed. Susan Lohafer and Jo Ellyn Clarey (Baton Rouge: Louisiana State University Press, 1989), 8.

63. Charles E. May, "The Nature of Knowledge in Short Fiction," *Studies in Short Fiction* 21 (Fall 1984): 227–38.

64. Mary Louise Pratt, "The Short Story: The Long and the Short of It," *Poetics* 15 (1981): 175–94.

65. Walter Allen, *The Short Story in English* (Oxford, Eng.: Clarendon Press, 1981).

66. Valerie Shaw, *The Short Story: A Critical Introduction* (London: Longman, 1983).

67. Helmut Bonheim, *The Narrative Modes: Techniques of the Short Story* (Cambridge, Eng.: D. S. Brewer, 1982).

68. John Gerlach, *Toward the End: Closure and Structure in the American Short Story* (Tuscaloosa: University of Alabama Press, 1985).

69. John Bayley, *The Short Story: Henry James to Elizabeth Bowen* (New York: St. Martin's Press, 1988); Clare Hanson, *Short Stories and Short Fictions, 1880–1980* (New York: St. Martin's Press, 1985).

70. *The Teller and the Tale: Aspects of the Short Story*, ed. Wendell M. Aycock (Lubbock: Texas Tech Press, 1982); *Re-Reading the Short Story*, ed. Clare Hanson (New York: St. Martin's Press, 1989).

71. Suzanne Hunter Brown, "'Tess' and *Tess*: An Experiment in Genre," *Modern Fiction Studies* 28 (1982): 25–44; Suzanne Ferguson, "Defining the Short Story: Impressionism and Form," *Modern Fiction Studies* 28 (1982): 13–24.

72. Frederic Jameson, *The Prison-House of Language* (Princeton: Princeton University Press, 1972), 73.

73. See Roland Barthes's study of a Balzac short story in *S/Z* (New York: Hill and Wang, 1974); and Tzvetan Todorov's studies of various short forms in *Poetics of Prose* (Ithaca: Cornell University Press, 1977).

74. Seymour Chatman, "New Ways of Analyzing Narrative Structure, with an Example from Joyce's *Dubliners*," *Language and Style* 2 (1969): 3–36; Gerald Prince, *A Grammar of Stories: An Introduction* (The Hague: Mouton, 1973).

75. Susan Lohafer, *Coming to Terms with the Short Story* (Baton Rouge: Louisiana State University Press, 1983).

76. Susan Lohafer, "A Cognitive Approach to Storyness," *Short Story*, Spring 1990, 60–71; "Preclosure and Story Processing," in *Short Story Theory at a Crossroads*, 249–75.

77. Charles E. May, *Fiction's Many Worlds* (Lexington, Mass.: D.C. Heath, 1993).

78. Charles E. May, "Teaching Narrative Literacy with Toolbook Short Story," *THE Journal* Supplement, January 1992, 10–12.

79. For the complete text of a number of the critical essays mentioned in this chapter, as well as an extensive annotated bibliography of short story theory and criticism, I refer the reader to the revised edition of *Short Story Theories*, ed. Charles E. May (Athens: Ohio University Press, 1994) entitled *The New Short Story Theories*.

Recommended Titles

S hort stories maintain their popular interest and critical importance by being included in college textbook anthologies and
by being explicated and analyzed by critics. The following list of
over one hundred stories represents the most influential and
important short stories in the history of the form as determined
by these two criteria. Dates of original book publication of the
stories may be found in the Chronology. The annotations focus
on critical, historical, or generic significance of the individual
works.

Achebe, Chinua, "Dead Men's Path." A brief but powerful story about
   the clash between tribal values and the encroachment of "progres-
   sive" education in Africa.
Aiken, Conrad, "Silent Snow, Secret Snow." Both a case study in schizo-
   phrenia and an aesthetic fable about the retreat from reality into
   the perfection of art.
Aldrich, James, "Marjorie Daw." A popular late-nineteenth-century trick-
   ending story that focuses on the relationship between reality and
   ideality.
Anderson, Sherwood, "Death in the Woods." Anderson's best-known
   treatment of his own storytelling technique, this is a self-reflexive
   tale about the power of story.
Anderson, Sherwood, "Hands." Often described as the most subtle and
   symbolic story in his influential *Winesburg, Ohio* collection.
Anderson, Sherwood, "I'm a Fool." Another of Anderson's first-person
   stories of a young man's initiation into the inevitable ambiguities
   of adult life.

Anderson, Sherwood, "I Want to Know Why." One of Anderson's best-known first-person initiation stories, which emphasizes the discovery of adult reality's complexity.

Babel, Isaac, "My First Goose." Babel's best-known treatment of his fascination with the violence of military life.

Baldwin, James, "Sonny's Blues." A sophisticated attempt to communicate the nature of the African American tradition, racial identity, brotherly relationships, and the essence of the blues.

Bambara, Toni Cade, "The Lesson." One of Bambara's most popular stories, it is significant for its thematic treatment of economic discrimination by means of a wisecracking narrator.

Barth, John, "Lost in the Funhouse." The best-known story from Barth's collection of the same name, it typifies his interest in the relationship between reality and the world of the artwork.

Barthelme, Donald, "The Balloon." One of Barthelme's most popular satires about the relationship between the artwork and the observer/reader.

Barthelme, Donald, "A Shower of Gold." One of Barthelme's most influential early stories, it introduced readers to his sophisticated satire of many of the icons and ideals of modern culture.

Beattie, Anne, "Janus." Typical of Beattie's work for its focus on a middle-class woman and subtle treatment of a central symbolic object.

Bierce, Ambrose, "An Occurrence at Owl Creek Bridge." The shocking trick ending of this story often obscures its subtle treatment of the nature of fictional time.

Borges, Jorge Luis, "Funes the Memorious." A well-known example of Borges's usual metaphysical-aesthetic focus: Funes's inability to forget anything makes it impossible for him to abstract from his experience.

Borges, Jorge Luis, "Pierre Menard, Author of *Quixote.*" Borges's story about the man who rewrites Cervantes's *Don Quixote* is a parable about the intertextuality of literature.

Boyle, T. Coraghessan, "Greasy Lake." Boyle's comic grotesque story hovers between the real world and nightmare.

Camus, Albert, "The Guest." Of the few stories Camus wrote, this one has been very influential for its stark presentation of his absurdist view of reality.

Capote, Truman, "A Tree of Night." Capote's most famous early story about the grotesque and inextricable mix of dream and reality.

Carver, Raymond, "Cathedral." Carver's most famous story from his later period; more discursive and detailed in technique and more optimistic and hopeful in theme than his earlier, starker stories.

Carver, Raymond, "Why Don't You Dance?" A minimalist story typical of Carver's early period, it emphasizes the Chekhovian use of concrete details to communicate hidden reality.

Cather, Willa, "Paul's Case." Both a realistic treatment of the suffocation of middle-class life in America and an ambiguous parable of escape into aesthetic reality.

Cheever, John, "The Country Husband." One of Cheever's best-known stories about the midlife crisis of a suburban middle-class man.

Cheever, John, "The Enormous Radio." Cheever's best-known story combination of fantasy and reality.

Cheever, John, "The Swimmer." Cheever's best-known example of his typical technique of combining realism and fantasy and his typical theme of the midlife crisis of the middle-class suburban man.

Chekhov, Anton, "Gooseberries." Chekhov's most frequently anthologized story, about the ironic nature of self-deception and his own narrative technique.

Chekhov, Anton, "The Lady with the Pet Dog." One of Chekhov's most subtle stories about the inevitable gap between public and private reality.

Chekhov, Anton, "Misery." An excellent example of Chekhov's treatment of the inexpressibility of powerful feelings.

Chopin, Kate, "Désiree's Baby." Chopin's most successful story is still her most popular, especially with feminist critics: it combines serious social criticism with an ironic trick ending.

Conrad, Joseph, "The Secret Sharer." Conrad's most famous symbolic story in which the psychic self is projected into the world of the story.

Coover, Robert, "The Babysitter." A highly stylized experiment with narrative point of view; one of the best-known examples of the so-called modern "anti-story."

Crane, Stephen, "The Blue Hotel." Crane's most famous symbolist tale focuses on the conflict between fictional reality and external reality in a classical tragic structure.

Crane, Stephen, "The Bride Comes to Yellow Sky." Sophisticated comic satire of the popular western story of the nineteenth century.

Crane, Stephen, "The Open Boat." Crane's starkest treatment of the existential confrontation with nature's indifference and the affirmation of the community of human life.

Defoe, Daniel, "A True Relation of the Apparition of One Mrs. Veal." Historically important for its early combination of the supernatural subject matter of the tale and the realistic technique of the eighteenth-century novel.

Dinesen, Isak, "Sorrow-Acre." Dinesen's best-known treatment of her common theme of the aristocratic code by which people preserve beauty by making life into an elegant game.

Doyle, Arthur Conan, "The Adventure of the Speckled Band." One of the best-known Sherlock Holmes stories; particularly interesting for its focus on the readerly interpretation of clues by the detective figure.

Faulkner, William, "Barn Burning." Faulkner's best-known initiation story focuses on the tension between family allegiance and abstract ideals.

Faulkner, William, "A Rose for Emily." A Gothic horror story and a fable about the American South and an ambiguous combination of tragic stature and comic effect.

Fitzgerald, F. Scott, "Babylon Revisited." Fitzgerald's best-known story about the aftermath of the Jazz Age.

Freeman, Mary Wilkins, "A New England Nun." A famous local color story that challenges the genteel tradition.

García Márquez, Gabriel, "A Very Old Man with Enormous Wings." García Márquez's most popular example of his "magical realism"—the presentation of fantastic events in the most commonplace surroundings and matter-of-fact tone.

Gass, William H., "In the Heart of the Heart of the Country." Gass's most popular lyrically self-reflexive treatment of the nature of storytelling.

Gilman, Charlotte Perkins, "The Yellow Wallpaper." A late-nineteenth-century feminist story rediscovered in the 1980s that focuses on the difference between the texts of women and the texts of men.

Glaspell, Susan, "A Jury of Her Peers." Although this story has been around for some time, the rise of feminist criticism has revived it; the feminist theme is developed by means of detective story conventions.

Godwin, Gail, "A Sorrowful Woman." A chilling modern fairy tale about one woman's discovery that she cannot tolerate her predetermined role as wife, mother, housekeeper.

Gogol, Nikolai, "The Overcoat." Gogol's famous and influential grotesquely comic treatment of the "little man."

Gordimer, Nadine, "The Train from Rhodesia." The social conflict between native art and the commercialism of colonial whites in South Africa is intertwined with one woman's discovery about love and understanding.

Greene, Graham, "The Basement Room." Greene's best-known initiation story focuses on the nightmarish world of the child and the discovery of evil and individual responsibility.

Harte, Bret, "Tennessee's Partner." Harte's deceptively simple story of one man's devotion to another is actually an ironic comedy in the western tradition.

Hawthorne, Nathaniel, "My Kinsman, Major Molineux." An extremely complex Hawthorne initiation story that makes use of his typical combination of dream and reality.

Hawthorne, Nathaniel, "Rappaccini's Daughter." Hawthorne's most complex story about the ambiguous nature of evil.

Hawthorne, Nathaniel, "Young Goodman Brown." Hawthorne's combination of allegory with psychological verisimilitude makes this one of his most influential contributions to the development of the short story.

Hemingway, Ernest, "Big Two-Hearted River." The best example of Hemingway's transformation of ordinary everyday objects and events into projections of psychic distress.

Hemingway, Ernest, "A Clean, Well-Lighted Place." One of Hemingway's shortest, most cryptic, and most philosophical stories, it emphasizes confrontation with the existential notion of nothingness.

Hemingway, Ernest, "Hills Like White Elephants." Hemingway's most compressed and unified story is an excellent example of his stylized dialogue and subtle symbolism.

Hemingway, Ernest, "The Killers." Hemingway's famous initiation story about the discovery of evil through confrontation with comically stereotypical gangsters.

Henry, O., "The Gift of the Magi." O. Henry's most famous trick-ending story about the poor couple at Christmas who sell their most precious possessions to give a gift to each other.

Hoffman, E. T. A., "The Sandman." Important German romantic treatment of the inextricable mix of reality and fantasy.

Hurston, Zora Neale, "Spunk." An African American folktale, complete with larger-than-life heroes and supernatural interventions.

Irving, Washington, "The Legend of Sleepy Hollow." Irving's combination of a European folktale with an American setting and an urbane teller makes this an innovative early short story.

Irving, Washington, "Rip Van Winkle." Irving's famous story about the man who sleeps through adulthood is an early example of the American short story's combination of folktale and social satire.

Jackson, Shirley, "The Lottery." One of the best-known stories in American literature, primarily because of its creation of a realistic-mythic world and its shocking ending.

James, Henry, "The Beast in the Jungle." James's complex story of the human mind's self-deception and modern man's retreat from action into thought.

James, Henry, "The Real Thing." James's most frequently anthologized story is a sophisticated treatment of the relationship between reality and representation.

Joyce, James, "Araby." The best-known initiation story from Joyce's *Dubliners*, it focuses on the young male protagonist's idealization of a girl and his epiphanic realization of his foolishness.

Joyce, James, "The Dead." Joyce's most famous and most subtle story is the best example of his transformation of realistic detail into symbolic significance.

Kafka, Franz, "A Country Doctor." Kafka's most ambiguous story has elicited social, psychological, philosophical, and theological interpretations.

Kafka, Franz, "The Hunger Artist." One of Kafka's most frequently anthologized stories, it is a parable of an artist of the negative that pushes Poe's theme of aesthetic reality to fantasy extremes.

Kafka, Franz, "The Metamorphosis." Kafka's best-known example of his realistic treatment of the most fantastic events.

Kipling, Rudyard, "The Man Who Would Be King." One of Kipling's most admired stories; an ironic treatment of the transformation of men into mythic reality.

Lardner, Ring, "Haircut." One of the best-known ironic dramatic monologues in American short fiction.

Lawrence, D. H., "The Horse-Dealer's Daughter." The best short story example of Lawrence's symbolic technique and his typical theme of the power of physical desire.

Lawrence, D. H. "The Rocking-Horse Winner." Lawrence's best-known psychological fairy tale about childhood fantasy and adult needs and failures.

London, Jack, "To Build a Fire." London's naturalistic story about one man's confrontation with the indifference of nature.

Malamud, Bernard, "The Magic Barrel." One of the best stories from Malamud's prizewinning collection of the same name, it is a fine example of his mixture of myth and reality.

Mann, Thomas, "Disorder and Early Sorrow." Mann's best-known ironic treatment of the bourgeois world in dissolution.

Mansfield, Katherine, "The Fly." One of Mansfield's most ambiguous Chekhovian stories about the oblique communication of emotions that evade statement.

Mansfield, Katherine, "The Garden Party." One of Mansfield's most delicate symbolic initiation stories, it focuses on a young girl's ambiguous discovery of class differences and of the beauty and ugliness of death.

Mason, Bobbie Anne, "Shiloh." One of the most popular stories by one of the best-known practitioners of "K-mart realism," in which working-class men and women face a subtle conflict.

Maupassant, Guy de, "Madame Tellier's Excursion." One of Maupassant's best realistic stories, it is more representative of his art than his better known ironic trick-ending stories.

Maupassant, Guy de, "The Necklace." Maupassant's best-known ironic trick-ending story.

McCullers, Carson, "A Tree, a Rock, a Cloud." McCullers's best-known story focuses on the complex nature of human love.

Melville, Herman, "Bartleby the Scrivener." Melville's masterpiece about Bartleby, the scrivener that would "prefer not to," bridges the generic gap between the old tale form and the new realism.

Mérimée, Prosper, "Mateo Falcone." Often referred to as the first modern French short story, it combines romantic folk tale subject matter with realistic techniques.

Nabokov, Vladimir, "Signs and Symbols." Nabokov's most famous self-reflexive story focuses on the nature of fictional reality and the reader's relationship to it.

Oates, Joyce Carol, "Where Are You Going, Where Have You Been?" One of Oates's most popular stories, it focuses on a young woman's confrontation with evil; her technique combines realism and fantasy.

O'Connor, Flannery, "Good Country People." A typical O'Connor treatment of the southern grotesque and the extremity of the Christian need to lose the self in order to find it.

O'Connor, Flannery, "A Good Man Is Hard to Find." O'Connor's most shocking example of her usual theme of the violence of redemption and the recognition of the self.

Olsen, Tillie, "I Stand Here Ironing." The rise of feminist criticism made this a very popular story in the 1980s; the first-person point of view casues a complex value reaction in the reader.

Ozick, Cynthia, "The Shawl." A powerful symbolic tale of the Holocaust, in which the horror of millions is communicated by the silence of one individual.

Paley, Grace, "A Conversation with My Father." Paley's attempt to write a story of which her father will approve—about storytelling, generational attitudes, and history.

Poe, Edgar Allan, "The Cask of Amontillado." The best example of Poe's insistence that short stories must be unified around a single effect: a tightly structured, ironic story quite dependent on point of view.

Poe, Edgar Allan, "The Fall of the House of Usher." Poe's classic tale of the romantic artist's ultimate detachment from external reality.

Poe, Edgar Allan, "The Murders of the Rue Morgue." Often called the first detective story, this famous tale introduces Dupin, Poe's combination of artist/reader detective.

Poe, Edgar Allan, "The Purloined Letter." Because of its focus on textuality, this Poe detective story has been the subject of a great deal of modern criticism and theoretical speculations.

Poe, Edgar Allan, "The Tell-Tale Heart." Poe's most complex study of the relationship between psychological obsession and his own theory of aesthetic unity.

Porter, Katherine Anne, "Flowering Judas." Porter's most famous symbolic story about a woman's refusal to make a human commitment.

Porter, Katherine, "The Grave." Porter's most compressed and symbolic story focuses on her usual themes of memory and initiation.

Pushkin, Alexander, "The Queen of Spades." Marking the beginnings of the Russian short story, it combines old supernatural tale with modern ironic story.

Roth, Philip, "The Conversion of the Jews." Frequently anthologized comic initiation story about a young man's conflict with his elders and his religious beliefs.

Silko, Leslie Marmon, "Yellow Woman." This is a typical Silko blend of American Indian myth with the fantasies of modern-day woman.

Singer, I. B., "Gimpel the Fool." Singer's famous ironic story about the wise fool who transcends reality by his innocent gullibility.

Steinbeck, John, "The Chrysanthemums." One of Steinbeck's most popular stories from his collection *The Long Valley*, it is a symbolic story with a feminist theme.

Steinbeck, John, "Flight." Steinbeck's mythic story about a young boy's escape from authorities and subsequent retreat to primitive human origins.

Stockton, Frank, "The Lady or the Tiger." In this famous trick-ending story the reader is asked to choose how the story will close.

Thurber, James, "The Secret Life of Walter Mitty." A slight but popular comic story about the power of daydreaming

Tieck, Ludwig, "Der Blonde Eckbert." This romantic transformation of the traditional fairy tale form foregrounds the thematic nature of fairy tales as revelatory of unconscious processes.

Tolstoy, Leo, "The Death of Ivan Ilych." Tolstoy's stark, realistic parable of man's confrontation with death and the meaninglessness of life lived on the conventional surface.

Turgenev, Ivan, "Bezhin Meadow." The best-known story from his influential *Sportsman's Sketches* collection, it is a lyrical treatment of the story-created world.

Twain, Mark, "The Celebrated Jumping Frog of Calaveras County." Twain's most famous tall tale is actually a parody of the tall tale form.

Updike, John, "A&P." A classic first-person initiation story in which the viewpoint of the young male narrator expresses the values of chivalric romance in contemporary adolescent slang.

Walker, Alice, "To Hell with Dying." A compressed, almost parabolic story about the persistence of life and the discovery of death.

Welty, Eudora, "Death of a Traveling Salesman." An excellent example of Welty's technique of combining fantasy and reality to create what she calls a "season of dreams."

Welty, Eudora, "Why I Live at the P.O." Welty's best-known first-person monologue is a comic exploration of schizophrenic split in the self.

Welty, Eudora, "A Worn Path." Welty's best-known mythic story is based on archetypal spiritual journey motif.

Williams, William Carlos, "The Use of Force." Using an experimental narrative method, Williams explores modern man's confrontation with, and rationalization for, his primitive urges.

Wright, Richard, "The Man Who Was Almost a Man." A very popular story about the transition of a young rural African American male from adolescence to adulthood.

Index

Barthelme, Donald, 20, *87–90*, 144;
"The Balloon," *87–88*, 144; *Come
Back, Dr. Caligari*, 87; "The
Indian Uprising" 88; "Me and
Mrs. Mandible," 89; "Robert
Kennedy Saved from
Drowning," 89; "See the Moon,"
88; "A Shower of Gold, 144
Barthes, Roland, 126
Bates, H. E., 17, 112
Baudelaire, Charles, 14
Baxter, Charles, "The Cliff," 90
Bayley, John, 125
Beattie, Ann, 20, 98, 99, 128; "Janus,"
99, 144
Bergonzi, Bernard: *The Situation of
the Novel*, 116, 117
Bierce, Ambrose: "An Occurrence at
Owl Creek Bridge, 11, 43, 80,
144
Blythe, Hal, 80
Boccacio, Giovanni: *The Decameron*, 2,
3, 111
Bolter, David, 127
Bonheim, Helmut, 125
Borges, Jorge Luis, 20, 54, *84–85*, 90;
"Funes the Memorious," 84,
144; "The Library of Babel," 85;
"The Lottery in Babylon," 85;
"Pierre Menard, Author of the
Quixote," 84, 144; "Tlon, Uqbar,
Orbis Tertius," 85
Bowen, Elizabeth, 125; *The Faber Book
of Modern Short Stories*, 123
Boyce, Benjamin, 4
Boyle, T. Coraghessan: *The Descent of
Man*, 90; *Greasy Lake and Other
Stories*, 91; "Greasy Lake," 91,
144; "The Hector Quesadilla
Story," 91
Brickell, Herschell, 115
Brontë, Emily: *Wuthering Heights*, 22
Brooks, Cleanth: *Understanding
Fiction*, 119, 121
Brown, Suzanne Hunter, 125
Browning, Robert: "Childe Roland to
the Dark Tower Came," 32
Burbank, Rex, 60

Cahan, Abraham, 52
Camus, Albert: "The Guest," 144
Canby, H. S., 7, 51, 52, 111, 113, 114,
120
Canterbury Tales, The, 111
Capote, Truman, 19, 77; "A Tree of
Night," 144
Carver, Raymond, 20, *91–97*; "The
Bath, 96–97," Cathedral," *94–96*,
144; "Errand," *104–6*;
"Neighbors," *92–93*; "A Small
Good Thing," 97; *What We Talk
About When We Talk About Love*,
93, 97; *Where I'm Calling From*,
94, 95, 97, 104; "Why Don't You
Dance?," *93–94*, 144; *Will You
Please Be Quiet, Please?*, 92
Cassirer, Ernst, 1, 2, 124
Cather, Willa, 81; "Paul's Case,"
145
Cervantes, Miguel de, 22, 84;
Exemplary Novels, 3
Chatman, Seymour, 126
Cheever, John, 19, 80; "The Country
Husband," 80, 145; "The
Enormous Radio," 80, 145; "O
Youth and Beauty," 80; "The
Swimmer," 80, 145; "Torch
Song," 80
Chekhov, Anton, 15, 16, 18, 20, 30,
45, *51–56*, 60, 61, 63, 66, 68, 70,
71, 72, 77, 81, 91, 92, 94, 97, 100,
104–6, 145; "Gooseberries," 38,
53–55, 66, 145; "The Lady with
the Pet Dog," 145; "Misery," 16,
53, 54, 56, 145
Chekhovian, 18, 20, 52, 56, 62, 63, 67,
69, 80, 97, 98, 99, 144, 148
Chicago critics, 121
Chopin, Kate, 81; "Desireé's Baby,"
145
Clarey, Jo Ellen: *Short Story Theory at
a Crossroads*, 124, 125
closure, 44, 57, 125
cognitive science, 127
Coleridge, Samuel Taylor, 7
Conrad, Joseph, 12, 15, *47–50*, 55,
108, 145; *Heart of Darkness*, 32,

About the Author

Charles E. May is probably the best-known and most frequently quoted expert on the short story genre. He has published a number of scholarly books on the topic: *Short Story Theories*, *The Modern European Short Story*, *Edgar Allan Poe: A Study of the Short Fiction*, *Fiction's Many Worlds*, and *The New Short Story Theories*—and over 200 articles to such journals as *Studies in Short Fiction*, *Style*, and *The Minnesota Review*. May is professor of English at California State University, Long Beach. Other academic positions he has held include president of the California State University English Council, and chairman of the C.S.U.L.B. English Department.